M000213771

THE CRYSTAL MAGIC SPELL BOOK

A BEGINNER'S GUIDE FOR HEALING, LOVE, AND PROSPERITY

BRIDGET BISHOP

HENTOPAN
PUBLISHING

CONTENTS

Get this additional book free just for joining the Hentopan Launch Squad.

If you want insider access, plus this free book, all you have to do is scan the code below with your phone!

INTRODUCTION

For centuries, the practice of magic and witchcraft has had a bad rap. Stereotyping and stigma, linking witchcraft to devil worshiping and other unflattering depictions, are finally falling by the wayside. Nowadays, practicing magic has developed into an appealing and modern belief system. One such type of specialized magic is used for attracting that special person. While love spells do seem contemporary, they date back to ancient times. Between the 1400s and the 1700s in the United Kingdom, witchcraft was continuously honored by some villagers who would frequently visit those who were believed to practice witchcraft with their problems related to love, marriage, and attraction. At that time, and still today, love spells are cast in the form of rituals, potions, written text, or by utilizing items such as candles or dolls.

More than ten years ago, after a bad break-up with my partner and losing my job, I felt as if my life was spiraling out of control. I wanted to get back on a spiritually positive path and regain my self-worth. I was introduced to magic by a close friend. Just some basic magical spells and rituals; a way to distract myself from my woes. I never imagined that I would not only regain control over my emotions, but also the power to be the captain of my own ship and the master of my destiny. Like Humpty Dumpty, I was put back together again. I was first attracted to crystals as a young child, when my mom took me with her to a small shop. I felt "pulled" towards a particular crystal and begged my mother to buy it. I then collected several more as I grew up, long before I knew anything about magic. Today, I believe crystals were my "gateway drug" into magic and have come to realize that crystals are like that for many people. Most who believe in the healing powers of crystals have come to realize they are practicing magic. The spells set forth in this book will help you to learn how to harness your magical powers and amplify the potential power of crystals.

Mineral stones and crystals are extremely versatile and surprisingly powerful tools of magic. Practitioners of modern magic use crystals for more than just divination; they are used for attracting love, gaining wealth, improving health, and much more. If you have ever picked up a crystal and held it up to the light, looking closely as you turn it over and inspect its wonder from all different angles, you can't help but notice the mysterious sense of awe evoked by these special stones. The word "crystal" means any substance formed naturally by geological processes under the Earth's ground. Each one has its own unique chemical composition, along with its own magical energy signature. The most familiar crystal stone is probably clear quartz. This is what real or true "crystal balls" are made from. Next comes amethyst and rose quartz. Other stones commonly used for magic include jade, bloodstone, and lapis lazuli, which are made from a combination of more than a single mineral and therefore are not considered to be "true" crystals. Other stones referred to as crystals, such as jet and amber, are actually organic substances that over time have become fossilized, rather than stones. For the sake of simplicity, most people who practice crystal magic use the term stones and crystals interchangeably.

While crystals are classified as inorganic, many who practice magic think of them as "alive" because they provide healing energy to all living things. Scientists call the effects of tourmaline and quartz piezoelectric because, when tapped by a hammer, they radiate an electric charge observable to the human eye. This is clear evidence of their innate energy and power. Magical practitioners understand that the crystal's power is the same as the power naturally occurring in the wind or flowing waters. All of energy, both seen and unseen, is interconnected. Since our intentions and thoughts are also forms of energy, we can use crystals as conduits to send positive energy and healing powers out into the universe. These energies come back to us in the spiritual realm and bring with them healing and positive vibes, manifesting as real change in our lives.

I

UNDERSTANDING CRYSTAL MAGIC

Crystals are natural elements that vibrate with their own magical resonance, and that resonance can be used in your magic. Their vibrations can heal, bring balance, and help you to reorganize the universe according to your will. But before you can jump into casting spells, you'll need to understand and take to heart some basic crystal magic knowledge.

1

THE MAGIC OF CRYSTALS

Once upon a time, crystals were considered "hippy" nonsense, and were dismissed as such. Nowadays, it seems that mysticism has gone mainstream. Crystals are embellishing everything from handbags to fine jewelry. The wellness industry has a huge global presence and includes crystals that have found their place in the everyday routine of alternative and complementary healthcare and fitness. Their physical attributes make crystals stand out, as they have the unique qualities that refract light and give it a dark, yet transparent appearance. This is part of the reason people from many different societies and cultures ascribe magical powers to them. There are many differing types of crystals, each with their own unique abilities to heal you physically, emotionally, and spiritually. They are known to enhance the flow of positive energy and help clear the mind and body of negative energy for emotional and physical benefits. Acceptance, reflection, and mindfulness are the key ingredients to indulging in this experience of wellness and self-care.

Historically, crystals are referenced all the way back to the Ancient Sumerians, who used them in their magic formulas. Turquoise, emeralds, quartz, and carnelian adorned the Ancient Egyptians and their amulets, while they also used peridot and topaz to rid the body of evil spirits and for other forms of protection and good health. Emeralds have been utilized throughout history, including in ancient Mexico, as a symbol of the heart of the dead, and were included in burials. The origin word 'crystal' is from Greek, meaning ice. It was thought at the time that clear quartz was water so frozen that it would never thaw. Likewise rooted in Greek origin is the amethyst, meaning "sober," which was often worn to prevent hangovers and drunkenness! You would think the world would be sold out of amethysts! Stemming from the Greek word for blood, "hematite" was worn by soldiers and sailors while preparing for and during battle, and to keep them safe at sea because of its reddish color. In ancient China, jade was of great value due to its healing properties, especially for kidney stones. It is still revered today. Jade is also considered to be very lucky in New Zealand and in other parts of the world where the tradition of the lucky stone has been passed down through generations. Knowing how different cultures perceived crystals throughout history tells us why we are so fascinated with them to this day.

Consider how I perceive my own collection, in layman's terms: when I hold my citrine crystal, it reminds me to check in with my intentions and to hit head-on any obstacles that may be in my way. Even if you are new to crystal vibrational energies, just remember that it is about gaining the highest self-awareness and finding balance in your life. It is not about simply buying a few beautiful crystals and speaking some magical words over them. It is about building a personal relationship and a connectedness with them if you want them to successfully work with you.

Why Crystals are a Great Place to Start with Magic

Crystals are powerful healing agents because they permit fruitful and positive vibrations to flow into the body and take the negativity and toxic energy away. They work by channeling your vibrational energy levels to focus on healing your body from its core. Each crystal has its own unique frequency and vibration, arising from their composition on a molecular level. The way the crystal's molecules interact and create energies and vibrations is behind the beneficial aspects they provide. Crystals are magnets that absorb negative energies and enhance positive vibes. Because they are created naturally, they harness the energies of the oceans, the moon, and the sun and use those energies for healing, lifting our moods, and improving our overall state of being. When you hold a crystal in your hand it interacts with the chakras in your body and enhances emotional and physical wellness. Crystals vibrate at the same frequencies as you and I and help the healing abilities already within us to reach their full potential. This comfort provided by the stones, when placed on your body, helps you to feel protected and at ease.

Crystals' Vibrational Energy

Making a personal connection with your crystals and gems is one of the essential elements of working with them. Learning how to feel and recognize the crystal's energy is how you establish and strengthen your connection. If you are just starting out, here are a few tips: work with a crystal that has been freshly charged and cleansed to feel the strongest energies. You can cleanse and charge your crystal with sage, sunlight, Palo Santo, dirt, and water. There is no "wrong" or "right" way to sense or feel the energy of your crystal. It has to feel right to you. You are the best avenue for discovering your deep connection to crystal energy over time. Depending on your connection and familiarity with the crystal, the energy can be very powerful or very subtle. Try not to feel disappointed or frustrated if you do not feel anything right away. When it is subtle, crystal energy can be difficult to discern or recognize during the first few times you try. Like everything worthwhile in life, it takes practice. The more you practice and focus on making a connection, the easier it will become to sense the crystal.

Here are some quick tips for your "vibes to rise" and for you to feel energy:

1. Set aside preconceived notions.
2. Take off any other crystal jewelry (including your engagement or wedding rings). It is much easier to feel the crystal's vibration if you are only focusing on one stone.
3. Remove or turn off all distractions, such as your cell phone, tv, radio, etc.
4. Start with one that attracts you.
5. The crystal will resonate with your own natural frequencies!
6. Close your eyes. Meditate before holding the crystal.
7. Take several deep breaths through your nose and exhale slowly out of your mouth while visualizing the energy of the crystal with each breath.
8. First start by rubbing your hands together to prepare the energy centers in your palms.
9. Place the crystal in your non-dominant hand or the one you feel is most receptive.
10. Spend a minute or two tuning into the crystal energy. Focus on your crystal and note any sensations you feel in your hands or anywhere in your body as you hold the crystal (starting with your hands). Notice any physical or emotional sensations.
11. Notice if the crystal feels cold or hot to your hand. Do

you feel any shaking, vibration, or buzzing from the crystal? Is your skin tingling? Concentrate on any feelings while focusing on your crystal. If you get goosebumps or chills, it is an indication that you are picking up the crystal's energy and vibrations.

12. Allow the energy to begin to take shape with each inhale and exhale, let it grow while you inhale its healing energy into every cell in your body, and exhale it back out to share its healing energy with the Earth.

13. Without any expectations for an outcome, let the crystal take you on a peaceful journey while filling you with its healing light.

14. While holding your crystal, focus on your mental state. Notice your experience; do you have clarity? Can you notice stress dissipating and anxiety decreasing? Let any negativity release itself from your body as you become more grounded. Be mindful of the moment.

15. Do you feel waves of relaxation or calmness, joy, love, protection? Perhaps you feel excited, positive, or motivated. If you feel sadness, know you are being healed. Just notice your feelings as you hold the crystal. Each crystal has its own unique properties and each one will have a different effect.

16. Remind yourself the crystal came from the Earth's heart and feel the connection.

17. Slowly, begin to open your eyes as you ease yourself

back into the material world (aka reality), becoming mindful of your surroundings.

18. Take a few slow breaths during this transition.
19. Look at and then thank your crystal.

Familiarizing yourself with each of your crystal's energies will tell you how that specific stone will help you in your life. When you find the crystal that helped you to relax, that will be the perfect stone to help you sleep or calm your nerves. If you notice feeling energized or motivated, this will be the crystal for enhancing your productivity. If you are having a rough day, choose the crystal that makes you feel comforted and loved. Trust what comes to your mind and continue to strengthen and grow in your connection to your crystals.

There is a growing body of evidence suggesting a strong connection between our bodies and our minds, so holding your crystal may first affect you physically; then as you focus on your stone, your emotions will start to change. With the ability to effect change in the vibrations in your body comes the power to better your physical health, change your mood (hopefully for the better), elevate your intentions, achieve your aspirations, and find peace through contentment. The experts in the field of vibrational energy know that certain emotions create specific vibrations. Joy, acceptance, and peace construct vibrations with high frequencies, while fear, hate, anger, and despair give off lower rate vibrations.

Hermetic principle #3:

"Nothing rests; Everything moves; Everything vibrates."

— THE KYBALION

Crystals vibrate at different frequencies depending on their matter, size, thickness, and their color (light frequency). The next step is to learn what stones resonate at the correct frequency for what you are trying to achieve. Thankfully, much experimentation has already been done for thousands of years by the ancients with the art of 'laying on of stones' and they've already figured out what stones help with what needs... for most. There are four scientific characteristics to crystal vibration: matter, color, size, and thickness. These attributes describe how the atoms and particles that make up all matter move in a back-and-forth motion. As previously mentioned, some thoughts and emotions have the highest vibrations, such as unconditional love and peace. To quote Tesla "If you want to understand the universe think in terms of energy, frequency, and vibration." The Hermetic principle #3 holds vibration as the driving force in understanding all creations in the universe. You may be wondering, "How do I sense my crystal's vibration?" The answer to this question is based on your degree of self-awareness. Are you experiencing grief, anger, or jealousy? If so, you may be in a low vibration emotional state. So, practicing how to shift your thoughts and emotions into a grateful high vibration is a good place to start. Different crystals react differently to different people - it depends on the person's own vibrational frequency and how it matches up with the crystal's vibrational frequency.

Daily Crystal Practice

1. Crystal magic is a part of daily self-care and will bring good feelings and balance into your life. Crystals will teach you to look inward for answers, how to go with the flow, and how to align your actions and thoughts with feelings associated with what you desire to attract. While you have hundreds of feelings at any given moment, it is your intuition that shows you which crystals, at that very moment, you need in your life. Carrying amethyst, selenite, and clear quartz with you on a daily basis will provide you with peace, stability, and receptiveness. All three have their own unique energies they radiate, and when together, they overlap in some places, which gives them heightened magical powers.

2. Smudge your crystal. Wave some burning juniper or sage, cedar, or mugwort over your crystal and in all of the corners of your space, leaving all of the doors,

windows, cabinets, and drawers open so that any lingering negativity finds a way out.

3. While holding your crystal, practice radical honesty about where you can recognize negative emotions. Take a look at any resentment you have and make the decision that it is time to let them go. They are dead weight anyway. You might be carrying around resentment as if it delivers some sort of punishment to the person who wronged you. That person, however, may never think about it and may be off traveling the world, having fun, or even winning the lottery. Isn't resentment a waste of time? Meanwhile, here you are with a dark spot in your heart and low frequency energy. Practice banishing these feelings with your crystal.

4. Finding clarity is important if you want to have a clear vision of what your heart desires and with what your intent is with your crystal ritual. With an open mind, imagine your desire as if you already have it. That way you can get rid of any thoughts blocking your way to success.

5. Practice a daily morning ritual. Spending a few moments aligning your energy right after you wake up in the morning sets the tone for the rest of your day. Choose your favorite ritual, such as a bit of yoga, positive affirmations, mindful meditation, etc. (something empowering). Next, prepare yourself for

your crystal ritual; set your intention and submerge yourself in that positive energy for what you want to happen for you during the day.

6. Make a habit of letting your creative juices flow when working with your crystal. Try to remember how it felt when you were a child and found awe in the smallest of things. Dance like nobody's watching, finger paint, color yourself creative in the kitchen. These are all good things. Consider this your energy-generated permission slip to dive into the world of positivity.

7. Your crystal practice is a way of treating yourself with kindness and love. Self-dialogue has a direct impact on how you feel. Get rid of negative self-dialogue, and even if you have to pretend at first, talk to yourself with compassion and understanding and your crystal will welcome the good vibes.

8. Along with getting to know your crystals, it is also important to lay off the toxins. Ridding your body of toxins will lift your vibrational energy. The more toxic an environment is, the harder it is to clean. The same goes for your mind and body. But when it comes to positive energy, put some thought into it. It will make a world of difference in your energy frequency communicated to your crystal.

9. Spiritual exercises are powerful ways of elevating your vibration. Connect with your crystal's energy and your

special spirit or "higher power" because it will help you know you are not alone and that you are loved and protected.

10. Avoid adopting someone else's low frequency vibrations. Taking on someone else's emotions is not the same as caring. You have the power within you to set boundaries and say to yourself, "Those are not my feelings."

11. Pause throughout your day and admire your crystals. Most of us have to-do lists that are a mile long. Practice some breathing techniques and don't forget to "stop and smell the roses." Einstein said, "He who does not pause to stand rapt in awe, is dead." Taking a short walk several times a day is a fantastic way to increase your frequency; it's like stopping to refuel your gas tank.

2

CRYSTAL BASICS

With a bit of gentle guidance, you can discover the wondrous powers of crystals. Learn how to cope with anxiety and stress and how to profile, select, and organize your own collection of crystals. Ever since that day my mother took me to the store and I begged her to buy me that stone, I have loved how just being around crystals makes me feel. Now, this passion is realized in every corner of my home and office. Some people like to use them for mental health or physical healing, some to find love, and others for prosperity. Some people just love to look at their beauty. Crystals are known to emit and store vibrations (or energy), as well as to amp up your own personal intentions and vibes. The best thing about doing magic with crystals is that there are no directions "set in stone" (pun intended). Just do what feels right to you.

Crystal Formation Experiment

Most crystals and other gems form because of forces that have been generating for billions of years. That is how many years it takes for hot magma to bubble from the center of the Earth and push its way to the top crust to form a mineral. Minerals then interlock, forming crystals. The rarest and finest crystals are polished after being cut and turned into gemstones. Some form as water evaporates and some grow inside of gaseous bubbles after the magma has pushed its way to the Earth's crust. Energy has always been here in some form or another; it cannot be created nor can it be destroyed but it can be transformed into another form of energy and here lies the magic of the crystal.

If you want to actually see crystals being formed, here is a little at-home experiment that is amazing.

1. Pour a ½ cup of water into a large cup or bowl.
2. Add ½ cup of Epsom salts to the water. (You can use table salt but it takes longer.)
3. Wait 24 hours.
4. As the water evaporates, the sodium atoms get closer together and form a cluster. They will keep coming together into a formation. This is the crystal you made yourself!

How Crystals Are Different from Gems, Minerals, and Rocks

Crystal is made from highly ordered and microscopic atoms that are naturally arranged to form a three-dimensional pattern also known by the term "crystal lattice." Billions of atoms form and shape the structure of the crystal in a process referred to as crystallization. Each mineral's crystal structure is fixed; should it change, it would not be the same mineral. The structure of the crystal defines the mineral variety. For instance, the structure of a quartz crystal will always be the same. Over time, some crystals grow quickly, while others can take millions of years, depending on how slow the magma cooling process is. The slower the cooling process, the bigger the crystal. Snowflakes can be made of a single crystal or they can be made of a collection of many crystals. When impurities infiltrate a crystal, it can affect the process of crystallization, and thereby create a change in color because its molecular makeup has been altered. Heat also alters the chemical process of crystallization and can also change its color.

Crystals have been heated by man for millennia, working to change or enhance their color. They can also be affected by a natural heating source such as the sun during their formation. Most of the finest gems in the world have been through some type of heating process. Gemstones are formed when a mineral or a piece of a rock is cut and often polished to be used in a piece of jewelry. That is how it becomes a gemstone. To be considered a gemstone, it must possess certain characteristics, such as rarity, durability, color, and beauty. Obviously, you can't just cut and polish any old rock and make it a gem. The four characteristics play an important role in their classification, with beauty being of the most importance. Many gemstones are cut from crystals.

Rocks are made from at least two different types of minerals bonded together. Granite and marble are two examples of rock. Rocks differ from crystals because they lack a crystalline structure.

The Meaning of the Shapes of Crystals

Crystals come in different colors (rose, amethyst, aquamarine) and are used for varying purposes, such as protection, attraction, health and wellness, sleep improvement, etc. But they are also formed into many differing shapes. The crystalline structure doesn't affect the type of energy it puts out; however, the shape of the crystal does affect the way you receive its energy. The shape of your crystal can help to ramp up your experience and your purpose. So, choosing the shape of a crystal should complement your intention and magnify and enhance your transformation.

Here are some of the crystal shapes and their influences:

1. Cubes

A cube-shaped crystal is the one you need if you're looking for some grounding energy. Placing a cubic crystal in your hands connects you to the vibrational energies of the Earth. You can also place them in each corner of your office or home for protection.

2. Pyramids

Pyramid-shaped crystals have very strong powers when it comes to manifesting your desires. This is because their strong base support works as an anchor for your intention. Its apex shape puts your intention out into the universe, whether it is for money or love. Pyramid crystals take it up a notch to fulfill your desire.

3. Spheres

Sphere-shaped crystals serve as a reminder that you are interconnected to all of the energies in your environment; part of a greater good; like imagining that you have the world in the palm of your hand. Sphere-shaped crystals give off a Zen vibe, making them perfect for meditation. Collecting a few small spheres to add to your crystal collection will assure your relaxation time will be special.

4. Tumbled Crystals

These are small and smooth crystals, considered to be the stepping stones into the magical world of vibrational energy. Don't let their small size fool you! The good news is they are travel-friendly and powerful indeed. You can take them with you anywhere you go; keep them close so you can reach out and grab them wherever you are and reconnect to their energy to be reminded of your intention all day long. They are like carrying around your best friend. I love them.

5. Crystal points

Points are powerful crystals that will keep you sharp-minded. A point crystal is the one to use when you need to stay super-focused on something. Pen your intention, desire, or affirmation on a sheet of paper. Fold up the paper and place it under your crystal point in a pyramid fashion. It will send all of the intention written on the paper upward and outward into the universe and into the atmosphere surrounding you.

6. Crystal hearts

Crystals that are heart-shaped have been cut and polished this way. They do not naturally occur but they still promote powerful love energy. Meditate on your intention and focus on a gentle loving light, filling your heart and clearing it of any old trauma, scars, or wounds; bring healing love and peace into your body.

7. Crystal Clusters

So beautiful are crystal points clustered together! They hold mystical vibrations and sparkle in their natural form. Put a crystal cluster on the coffee table, entranceway table, or dining room table, or on a conference table at work, to promote community and open-mindedness. I have one on my family dining table and it never goes unnoticed or without discussion, even though it has been there for years.

What is a Crystal Grid?

A crystal grid is a wonderfully powerful energy instrument to use when manifesting your intentions, goals, and desires. It is the way you arrange your crystals in a specific layout created for your exact intention. If you set your crystals up after much consideration and with intent, they are considered a grid. Just placing crystals near each other without a specific purpose is not considered a grid. If you are wondering why you should create a crystal grid instead of just using individual crystals, know that the grid power is derived from the union of energetic vibrations created between healing crystals. Using your intention to design a type of sacred geometrical pattern of crystals is an effective way to amplify their power. Using a crystal grid combines the power in the pattern you created, multiplying the crystals' energies. Working together, they will greatly strengthen their powers and your intention and bring about much faster results than you would be able to achieve using only single stones.

How to use a crystal grid depends on what your goal or intention is, as each grid can be designed for a different purpose or goal. Whatever your goal may be, you can create a powerful crystal grid to hold your intention and manifest it.

Step by Step Guide on Choosing the Shape of a Crystal:

1. Do a bit of homework about the vibrational and energetic characteristics of your crystal from a trusted source.
2. Consider your intent when selecting a shape that offers the benefits you are interested in.
3. Consider the way you are going to work with the crystal and where it will be stationed, such as on your altar, for chakra healing, or in a crystal grid.

The Colors of Crystals

The color of each crystal holds within it a vibrational energy, a specific intention, and an emotional response. The colors of the crystals are connected to the chakra system in our bodies, which refers to the energy centers corresponding to nerve bundles in our spine. It is inevitable that the stress of everyday life can throw your chakras out of balance. When this happens, it negatively affects you both physically and emotionally. Each chakra is associated with a color, beginning with purple at the top of your head down to red (the root chakra) at the base of your spine. These beautiful colors connected to the chakras have a deeper meaning; they are related directly to how each of the nerve bundles within that chakra functions.

By practicing with crystals in your meditations and rituals, you can enhance the magic of your present intentions and reap the effects you desire in your life. There are a multitude of crystals associated with every color known to man. My favorite way to bond with a new magical crystal is to let myself gaze through an assortment and notice where my eyes land first. You always know deep down inside what you need and your intuition leads you there. For starters, here are some of the colors I know well:

Red is an intense and powerful color that invokes our determination, passions, and inner strength. Red celebrates with us that we are alive! Red is connected to our root chakra and increases our self-confidence and courage, while releasing any lingering feelings of guilt and shame. When you need to pull out your warrior-self, use red to awaken your distinctive power and sensuality. When I am feeling the "go getter" in me, I wear my garnet earrings. Other red crystals include red calcite, cinnabar, sardonyx, rose quartz, and more.

Orange is a bit milder than red. It is a fun and flirty way to boost your creativity and motivate you toward success. It doesn't hurt to have it around in the bedroom too! If you really want to get your creative juices flowing, try a carnelian crystal. It is sure to do the trick. Orange crystals are associated with our sacral chakra and are the color of creation.

Yellow is obviously bright and happy. Yellow crystals provide new perspectives and a batch of clarity for when or if you are feeling confusion. Holding a yellow calcite will boost your confidence while clearing you of any self-doubt. Reach for a yellow crystal if your memory needs a quick boost or if you are attempting to learn a new skill.

Green is a color most of us could do with a bit more in our lives. It is connected to the heart chakra, as it facilitates abundance, healing, and nurturing. I love working with this vibrant shade along with others for a double dose of healing results. My favorite is malachite when my intention is focused on balance, money, manifestation, and transformation.

Blue is a favorite of many, as it represents total calmness. When holding a blue crystal, meditate on the vastness of the oceans and skies. It is associated with our throat chakra, and therefore, it works to enhance our communication skills and to clear up miscommunications from our lives. I love working with lapis lazuli when I am looking deep within myself for my inner truths and need clarification on how to appropriately communicate them to others.

Purple is associated with the crown chakra, and has a highly spiritual function, which serves to offer tranquility, enlightenment, protection, a good night's sleep, and enhanced intuition. Amethyst (Earth's natural tranquilizer) is the best-known purple crystal and possibly one of the most spiritually energetic stones to have in your collection. Other purple crystals include spirit quartz, lepidolite, charoite, and sugilite. Purple crystals relieve strain and stress while soothing irritability, alleviating grief, and diffusing negativity.

Clear and white clear away the mind's clutter and purify your thoughts and behaviors. White symbolizes cleanliness and purity. These crystals are perfect for new beginnings and for those just starting out with crystal magic, as white and clear crystals seem to be the easiest with which to work and connect. Whenever you have a need to promote peace and serenity or get a good night's sleep, use these crystals, ruled by the moon; its warm white rays of light will bring you tranquility.

Pink gives you a fuzzy warm feeling just by looking at it. Pink crystals carry a much more subtle power than red crystals. Their energy is loving, gentle, and warm, yet still provides you with the commitment, determination, and energy of the red crystals. Pink crystals carry with them energies of compassion, kindness, understanding, and love that everyone needs. Pink crystals will help you with the attributes of self-forgiveness or forgiveness for others, letting go of the mistakes of your past. They provide you with soothing emotional healing.

Aquamarine's properties include serenity, calm, and healing. It is fantastic for healing your stomach, liver, throat, and allergies. Also, it helps with pituitary and thyroid problems. To use aquamarine crystals, just place them over your throat for healing and for thyroid issues. Place over the brow to provide you with clarity, and over your heart to alleviate anxiety.

Agate's properties include vitality and strength. The color calms the stomach and helps with digestion. It also promotes psychological stability and balanced emotions. To use, simply keep it in your pocket, tucked in your bra, or in your purse where you can touch it often for strength.

Aventurine's properties include protection, anxiety reduction, and hopefulness. It comes in more than one color and works to relieve itchy skin and nausea and provide heart health and vision. Green aventurine quartz is used for economical abundance. To use, stick a green aventurine quartz in your pocket on your way to the casino or carry it in your purse for abundance and self-confidence. Hold it over your heart for blood pressure stability and heart health.

Rose quartz's properties include healing circulation, heart health and heartbreak, and fatigue. It also works to attract a new love interest or enhance the relationship you are in. It is also helpful for self-acceptance and self-care. To use it, keep it under your pillow in the bedroom. For heart health, place it on your chest while in a resting position. You can also hold it in your hand, rub your hands gently together and drop it in a glass of filtered water. Let it sit for one minute and then drink it.

Moonstone's properties include help with hormonal/menopausal problems, weight gain, joint pain, edema, migraines, and insomnia. To use moonstone, wear it as jewelry to stay safe during travel. You can also put it in the console on your car or under your pillow for a good night's rest.

Tourmaline comes in pink, black, brown, red, blue, yellow, colorless, or a combination of two or more of the above-mentioned colors. Tourmaline's vibrational energies depend on its color or combination of colors. Tourmaline crystals provide protection, grounding energy, and promote balance and stability. They are also useful for nerve damage, hearing problems, pain relief, flatulence, constipation, anxiety, and stress. Use it to absorb negative energy (make sure you clean it after use).

Clear quartz's properties include energizing, reducing anxiety and sensory nervous complaints, pain relief, calming respiratory issues, skin irritations, and congestion and swelling of mucous membranes. To use, carry in your pocket or purse, place under a pillow, meditate with it, decorate your home or office, give it as a gift, wear it as jewelry, or place it in your planters or in a sunny area just to relish in its beauty.

Shopping Tips for Crystals

As I mentioned, when I was 9 or 10 years old, my mother took me to a very cluttered antique shop, well hidden somewhere between my house and Timbuktu. I say Timbuktu because at the age of 9, anything more than 15 minutes in the car seemed like days. I didn't mind going to antique shops, because there were always interesting items, but none that I ever deeply felt a need to take home with me. However, this specific trip was anything but ordinary. I saw the glass case by the cash register and felt the most amazing pull towards this crystal. In the corner of the case were "the round ones." They were small spheres of crystal quartz, and believe it or not, I felt compelled to grab one. I immediately called my mother over to show her. All of a sudden, I felt drawn to a beautiful pink crystal. I told the lady behind the counter that I couldn't make up my mind which one I wanted. She said, "I'll make it much less complicated for you." She told me to "stick out my hands" and placed the clear crystal in one hand and the pink crystal in the other. She asked me to take a gander around the shop without thinking about holding the stones. Then she said, "Trust me, you will know today which crystal is meant for you to take home."

With that, I began looking around the shop. I remember admiring some Russian nesting dolls, all sorts of candles, long strings of beads, petrified pieces of wood, and wishing I could have them all. I continued to gaze around the shop while my mother was deciding which piece of artwork she wanted. Suddenly, I felt a strong electric shock run through my hand. I gasped. I figured it was somehow static electricity coming from the carpet I was walking on. All of the customers in the shop turned and looked at me like I had hurt myself. I asked the lady behind the counter if the crystals had batteries in them. She smiled at me and said, "Of course not; it looks like the pink crystal chose you."

It helps to learn a bit about the traditions of crystal healing vibrations and uses when it comes to shopping for a crystal. I have learned from my childhood experience to walk around the store and wait for the crystal to call out to me. If you feel a sensation from any of the crystals you are admiring, such as a tingle, pulse, peaceful feeling, or heat or cool sensations, this is a good indication that a crystal matches your needs. Make sure you don't overthink it. If you don't quite feel anything yet, pick out a few you love because of their beauty or uniqueness. Don't pick crystals based on the little information cards neatly stacked in front of them; just keep track of your collection. Once you get home you can do a bit of research on the ones you chose and you will find that they just so happened to be exactly what you needed.

3

CRYSTALS AND CHAKRAS

Some scholars in the Western world believe that the chakra system started around 1500 BC in India, when the earliest texts on yoga, the Vedas, were penned. Most of the scholars from India think the chakra system is very much older than that. In the chakra philosophy, the entire universe is acknowledged as being created, transfixed, and sustained by two perfect forces in a permanently indestructible union known as "Shiva" and "Shak" which are represented biologically as the feminine and masculine poles. The word chakra translates from Sanskrit to mean "wheel" and refers to the different energy points in the human body. They are thought of as spinning disks of energy that should stay aligned or "open" because they are associated with major organs, nerve bundles, and specific energetic areas of our bodies that affect our physical and psychological or emotional well-being. According to some, there are 114 different chakras in the human body, but seven of them are considered to be the main chakras which run along our spine. These seven chakras are the ones usually referred to in this manuscript.

Healing with Chakra Crystals

Each one of the seven main chakras is associated with a name, number, color, health focus, and a specific spinal area starting at the sacrum (just above the tailbone) and going to the top of your head, known as the crown. The sacrum energy is also known as the "root" chakra. Chakra crystals can be used in varying ways. Wearing jewelry adorned with them is an easy way to use them. Wearing a pendant of crystal can enhance your vibrational energy throughout the day. Carrying a crystal in a pocket or purse, somewhere where it is easy to touch, caress, or hold with a quick affirmation, works as well. Chakra crystals are also beneficial during healing practices. As you are meditating, rest one of your healing crystals just under your navel and it will bring increased focus and healing to your routine. If you are sitting and meditating, cup a crystal in your hands as you rest them in your lap for the same great outcome. Let's first take a look at the corresponding numbers and colors of the chakras before we go into the details of each one.

Chakras

#1 Root Chakra

#1 Root Chakra (Muladhara) is the first of the chakras, found at the base of the tailbone. It is important because, when balanced, it forms the base foundation for opening all of the chakras above it. Having a safe home means having a solid foundation upon which it can sit. If you want to live there for a while, you will need a firm foundation to provide the stability necessary to create a happy home for years to come. The root chakra is made up of whatever provides your stability in life; your grounding force. The root chakra comprises the basic human necessities, such as water, food, safety, and shelter. It is also responsible for your emotional well-being, including your ability to conquer fear. When aligned, you feel safe, grounded, and less worried throughout your day. Your root chakra has much to do with early childhood experiences because that is when it develops. If an individual has a traumatic childhood, they may find themselves in a root chakra blockage. If there is an imbalance in the root chakra, anxiety disorders, along with phobias and night terrors, as well as eating disorders, may develop. Physical imbalances can manifest as bladder and colon problems, lower extremity issues, and for men, prostate problems. When chakras are "out of whack," blocked, or misaligned, certain physical and emotional issues arise. If the root chakra is blocked, manifestations such as constipation, arthritis, urinary issues, and anxieties about basic needs and

money insecurities occur. When your root chakras open, you will feel secure and grounded, both emotionally and physically.

How to Balance #1 Root Chakra

Meditation and staying connected to your higher spiritual plane will help keep you grounded. You cannot always trust the outer world to provide you with safety or survival but you can trust in your spiritual self and in a power greater than yourself to provide you with emotional safety. It doesn't matter what name you give to that higher spirit; it can be Nature, God, or the Universe. If you think about it, animals are not positive when they will find food, but they do trust that Nature will provide. Smell is the sense organ associated with your root chakra.

> 1**Balancing Tip: Focus on the very tip of your nose while meditating and it will help in aligning your root chakra. The root chakra colors are red, black, and deep pink. Its crystals include hematite, garnet, ruby, black tourmaline, and black onyx.

#2 Sacral Chakra

#2 Sacral Chakra (Svadhisthana) is the second chakra and it is located in the lower abdominal area. It carries a few nicknames, including "the social chakra," "the creation chakra," and "the sex chakra." This chakra commands the reproductive organs and processes, sexuality, emotions, relationships, and your sense of adventure seeking. This chakra is concerned with much more than just sex. The reality is that it oversees pleasure and passion, not only by reproduction, but by creating other things, like beautiful artwork, music, or even your work, as well as just enjoying life. It does, however, govern sensuality, in the manner of embracing your own natural sexuality. Its crystal is the tiger's eye, its element is water, and its color is orange. When the sacral chakra is blocked or misaligned, urinary problems can pop up, as well as a loss of libido. Other reproductive issues can also arise, such as menstrual cramps accompanied by lower back pain. Emotionally, if your sacral chakra is blocked, you may feel closed off, ashamed of your sexuality, or plain old uncomfortable in your own skin. You may also feel a lack of creativity and find it difficult to pursue spontaneous endeavors. Fortunately, there are ways to conquer this and bring your sacral chakra back into alignment.

How to Balance #2 Sacral Chakra

First, exercises involving your hips can be beneficial in bringing balance back to your sacral chakra. Getting a hula hoop is a good idea, as it will help redirect your circulation and energy to the chakra, raising its vibrational energy. Of course, for all of the chakras, yoga and meditation are highly recommended. For realigning my sacral chakra, I perform the low lunge, goddess pose, and pigeon pose yoga asanas. Try your own yoga routine, such as yin yoga and creative yoga combined with affirmations to help keep your sacral chakra balanced and enhance your sensuality. Sound meditation works, too. Slowly let out the sound "vam" (or "lam" for your root chakra). This is pronounced like "lawn." Slowly, let the vocal vibrations seep through this area of your sacral chakra. This is a restorative and quick method for aligning your sacral chakra. Don't forget to practice affirmations as a powerful tool for balancing all of your chakras. For instance, for your sacral chakra, say "I am grateful for my body," "I accept myself," and "I am happy to be me." Another method for balancing and realigning your sacral chakra is aromatherapy.

The sacral chakra color is orange and it is associated with the moon, so orange and yellow crystals such as citrine (also good for cleansing) and orange carnelian are good for unblocking your sacral chakra or for opening it. Orange calcite also has cleansing characteristics which can open a blockage in your sacral chakra. Also, eating foods bright orange in color, such as sweet potatoes, carrots, and tangerines can help to restore balance to your sacral chakra. Moonstone crystals carry unique properties and they can soothe and open your sacral chakra. They are connected to the moon, which also governs the sacral region of the body! Since the moon controls the tides, if you want to become spiritually connected to your sacral chakra, spend some time at the beach, by a pond, river, or lake. These are relaxing locations that pair well with the feelings of adventure and pleasure with which the sacral chakra is associated.

#3 Navel or Solar Plexus Chakra

#3 Navel or Solar Plexus Chakra (Manipura) is set just behind your navel and governs your sense of purpose, confidence, self-worth, personal identity, and self-esteem. The Manipura is also associated with your metabolism and digestive system. When it is balanced and you have removed the negative aspects of your sacral chakra (Svadhishthana), you are aligned. As the foundation of digestive fire, the naval chakra oversees your pancreas and digestive tract; therefore, when it is blocked, a plethora of medical issues can arise. Ulcers, circulatory problems, diabetes, and hypertension are among them. However, when it is aligned, balanced, and strong it will help you to avoid these types of illnesses, as well as overcome them. The Manipura chakra balances your energy and keeps you healthy. When your Manipura is in good shape, you will feel confident, know who you are and what you want in life. The quality of your life will mean more to you than material gains; you will feel a sense of purpose. The emotional signs of a blocked #3 chakra can lead you into feeling powerless, removed, easily angered, controlling, and sometimes aggressive; it can also make you feel the opposite, feeling like a victim with low self-worth and neediness.

The colors of the third energy or naval chakra are golden or yellow, so any yellow or goldish crystals will open the Manipura. Tiger's eye, topaz, amber, yellow jasper, or yellow calcite are all good choices. Also, citrine is associated with abundance and good decision-making, and golden calcite helps with personal growth. Yellow is connected to a renewal of your nervous system and balance. Furthermore, it is the color of intellect. Manipura crystals draw their energies from the sun, and their frequencies connect to your conscious mind's frequency. If your self-confidence needs a boost, sport some amber earrings or yellow walking shoes. Aragonite crystals also come in yellow and are helpful for prosperity, concentration, and focus. Aragonite is a great grounding gem.

How to Balance # 3 Navel or Solar Plexus Chakra

The third chakra will help you find your truth - your authentic self. So, stepping outside of your comfort zone and trying something new is a great way to bring balance and open your solar plexus chakra. The word Manipura in Sanskrit means "city of jewels," so it is no surprise that it resonates with the element of fire and yellow crystals. It is the first relationship chakra, so placing a yellow crystal just below your navel while lying down will restore balance. Citrine crystals harness the energy of the sun, so using citrine as a healing stone will balance the energy of your solar plexus. Citrine broadens your perspectives about life; using it will raise your emotional vibration and give you the physical boost you need to remove any fears that may be holding you back in life. *Yellow jasper* is a naval chakra crystal that will encourage self-esteem and motivate you going forward. It is a crystal of protection that soaks up positive energy, providing you with more joy. Yellow jasper brings a sense of inner calmness and raises your stamina, giving you an uncanny ability to clear any misunderstandings that you may encounter.

#4 Heart Chakra

#4 Heart Chakra (Anahata) governs love, empathy, change, compassion, forgiveness, trust, peace, generosity, and gratitude. It is situated at heart level at the center of the spine. Anahata in Sanskrit means "unhurt." The fourth chakra is associated with the air element and is considered special because it is the exact middle point of the chakra system, so it acts as the spiritual and physical chakras' unifier. By connecting the lower three chakras (root, sacral, and navel) with the upper three chakras (throat, third eye, and crown) the heart chakra provides the connectedness between spirit and earth. Of course, its mantra is "I love." If your heart chakra is blocked or misaligned, you may feel a sense of unhappiness, insecurity, or as if your heart is broken and you are unlovable. You will be likely to distance yourself from your friends and put up emotional barriers, or become resentful, bitter, or even worse, totally shut down emotionally.

This is not a good chakra to have blocked; not that any of them are good to have blocked, but if you think about it, a blocked heart chakra is the worst because it makes you feel unloved and unlovable. However, if you're feeling a bit co-dependent, your heart chakra may be overactive. When your heart chakra is putting out too much vibration, it's in overdrive and causing an imbalance, which affects you in every way. It can leave you feeling emotionally bankrupt or lead you to toxic relationships. A heart chakra in overdrive can have you feeling ruled by your emotions. Believe me, everything is not okay when you are giving so much of yourself that you are neglecting yourself. Fortunately, there are methods for shaping up your heart chakra balance.

How to Unblock #4 Heart Chakra

The heart chakra has a unique frequency and its corresponding colors are pink and green. One might think that because it is the heart, the associated color would be red, but it is not. The fourth chakra symbolizes the ability to give and receive empathy, love, kindness, compassion, and healing, among other positive abilities. If you have an unbalanced Anahata, you might experience loss, pain, low self-esteem, or regret. Rose quartz crystals, jade, any of the pink or green crystals, green tourmaline, and green calcite attract love and open the heart chakra. You can wear jewelry, such as a rose quartz pendant, and experience its joy throughout your day. Display it in the corner of the tub when you bathe or conduct a healing session with it placed directly over your heart. As with all of the crystals, cupping a rose quartz in your hand while meditating will balance your heart chakra and remove any blockage. You can also create a grid with any of the heart chakra crystals if you want to attract a special someone.

#5 Throat Chakra

#5 Throat Chakra (Vishudha) is associated with self-expression (talking), truth, and communication (how you speak while expressing your emotions). The Vishudha is situated within the throat and neck area above the heart chakra in the body. This is your essential communication center where you store your vibrational energy for conscious dialogue and knowing how to strike a balance between speaking and listening. Having your throat chakra open is very important because communication is not only a necessary survival mechanism but it is also the key component of human interaction. You will know if your throat chakra is open when you express yourself with ease. A noticeable eloquence happens with an open and balanced throat chakra. You will have the ability to share your unique experiences, your perspectives on life and your valuable feedback with total confidence. The color associated with Vishudha is blue, due to its calming, honest, and empathetic properties.

How to Unblock #5 Throat Chakra

There are various ways to use crystals for opening, balancing, and aligning your throat chakra. Choose one of your blue crystals, such as amazonite, aquamarine, lapis lazuli, or the one you are most drawn to and lay them over your throat chakra (at the base of the throat) while meditating. You can also make your own jewelry. While focusing on your intention and holding two pieces of wire, twist them together in at least four twists, creating a V-shape at the bottom. Wrap wire around your blue crystal and make a loop at the top. It is that easy. Keep a crystal in your pocket for all-day energy. Amazonite will balance you emotionally and relieve your anxiety.

#6 Third Eye Chakra

#6 Third Eye Chakra (Ajna) is associated with your intuition, wisdom, and creativity. It is a vehicle for connecting you with different perspectives by opening your mind beyond the realm of the physical senses. It is difficult to put into words what it means to have a different way of seeing things because the visions are often subtle and involve the third eye. It takes some practice to sustain awareness of your Ajna chakra energy. Visions may be ghost-like or dreamy, cloudy, or blurry; however, at times they will be as clear as can be. The third eye chakra is situated on your forehead, between your eyes. The third eye chakra is connected to quintessential dimensions of the spirit world, those of wisdom, imagination, and truth.

How to Unblock #6 Third Eye Chakra

The third eye chakra is associated with the color of wisdom, purple. There are various crystals utilized during healing sessions for the Ajna. Sodalite is very helpful for procuring balance, focus, and mental clarity. It will keep you in a creative and calm head space when kept close by, such as on your desk or on the conference table. It is a violet-bluish color decorated with beautiful earth tones. For great penmanship, wear a sodalite ring. Don't be surprised to know I am wearing one right now to facilitate my creative writing skills. I just love it. When I started writing this book, there were so many wonderful aspects of crystal healing techniques running through my mind and so many directions in which the writing could flow. I found a royal blue sodalite crystal that had white calcium marbling. I had it set in silver and as soon as I slid it on my right ring finger, I felt a tingle throughout my whole body. My creative juices began to rush through me, and any writer's block I was experiencing seemed to fade away, as a sense of calmness and direction took over my fingers on the keyboard. This crystal has honestly made a difference in the way I express myself in writing.

#7 Crown Chakra

#7 Crown Chakra (Sahasrara) is situated at the very top of the head. It provides access to a higher state of being and opens you to things beyond your normal state of consciousness. What sets it apart from the other chakras is that it is actually just above the top of your head in what is considered to be your spiritual entity. It is not associated with a physical organ in the body, but with your consciousness. There are really no words to describe its unconditional love. Its color is white or indigo (light purple). However, when your Sahasrara is imbalanced, it can manifest itself in cynicism. When overactive, the opposite occurs and a feeling of closed-mindedness and disconnect from your body (living in your head) takes over.

How to Heal #7 Crown Chakra

The best way to heal your crown chakra is with your crystals. With access to the Sahasrara, your connection to the universe is made stronger. You acquire prana (pure life energy), which broadens your perspectives. You will also feel more motivated and highly spiritual. Here are some tips for using crystals to heal and/or balance your crown chakra. One of the best methods for healing your Sahasrara is through meditation.

Lay down and place a flat crystal on your crown (the top of your head). Amethyst is known for being a highly spiritual crystal and connects deeply with the crown chakra. It can calm the chaos in your mind and enlighten your soul to the spirit world. It takes you to the next level of spiritual development.

Lepidolite holds a gentle energy that connects on a deep level with the crown chakra. It does not open the chakra, but it will help you to stay calm during stressful times.

Clear quartz crystals are also known as master healers. They hold a high vibration with positive forces to bring about good health and wellness in all areas of your life. They awaken all of the chakras and can unblock your crown chakra and its beneficial energies. They will provide you with mental and spiritual clarity and improve your mental focus. Set your intention and time the first five minutes, while you hone your focus. Do this twice a day until you feel the healing process. Use this method to keep your crown chakra open and well-balanced.

Try using each of the above-mentioned crystals. I use clear quartz as a "winner take all" crystal because it makes me feel like all of my chakras open up as soon as I put it in my hands. Place a Sugilite crystal under your pillow. With its beautiful violet color, it has been used for thousands of years by healers and shamans.

Wear a moonstone in your hair. It will gently heal your crown chakra as it draws its energy from the moon.

4

ESSENTIAL CRYSTALS

Choosing the right crystal for spell work can be a bit confusing. Maybe you are just not sure about where to start. There can be so many reasons you want to take advantage of the healing powers of crystals in your life, and there is a plethora of crystals from which to choose. I use crystals every day of my life for healing and for my magical ventures. From amethyst to zebra jasper, choosing the right crystal is an amazing experience. Vibrational energies flow through and emerge differently according to the class of crystal you choose.

Your body will react accordingly to the unique properties and energies that crystals hold. Keep in mind that when picking the right crystal for your magic, one of the purposes of the crystal is to remind you of your deep connection to the earth's healing vibrations. Believing and focusing your intention on a particular crystal transmits that energy to the crystal you choose. This is the magic set in motion for your desired spiritual or physical healing. Think of crystals as your anchor to the Earth, always revealing themselves with universal healing characteristics and the elements of the world. They serve as wondrous aides and guides, inspiring and reinforcing our healing journey. Varying ailments require varying healing characteristics; therefore, some crystals are for protection while others are for balance, harmony, or love. Still others are for prosperity and clarity, and some are specific crystals with properties associated with alleviating health problems.

Now let's talk about balance. First off, balance is represented and deeply connected to the earth element. With how fast all of our emotions, thoughts, texting and typing, computing and overall emotional anxieties move nowadays, we have to somehow find balance by taking it easy and being mindful of our bodies. The concept of balance is dynamically ever-changing but needs a center point. So, if you are feeling out of balance, you need to check in with yourself over and over again, to find your center. We really can't discuss "balance" without talking about feminine and masculine energy. The whole world would be off kilter if it wasn't for the balanced yin yang or The Hermetic Principle of Polarity. Work your magic by balancing your chakras with your crystals and getting in touch with both your masculine and feminine energies. The same can be said about focusing on one type of magic. If you find yourself focusing on sun-powered magic, switch it up and spend some time with the Moon. The same goes for focusing on a single deity. If you have an element or god that you regularly work with, try learning how to work with a goddess too. You just need to experience balance; it doesn't mean you are holding the new goddess/god or element above the other.

The following are just thirty of the crystals I have the most experience using. I include the color, chakra, element, and magical uses of each of them:

1. AGATE

Colors: Brown, white, red, gray, pink, black, and yellow

Chakra: There is an agate for each of the chakras.

- Blue lace agate: throat chakra and the third eye chakra.
- Crazy lace agate: third eye chakra.
- Fire agate (red and brown): root chakra. Gold or orange fire agate: sacral chakra and solar plexus chakra. Green fire agates: heart chakra.
- Laguna agate: root chakra.
- Moss agate: heart chakra.

Element: Earth

Magical Uses: Speaking the truth, balancing between throat and heart chakras, loving unconditionally, living in peace and understanding.

2. AMBER

Color: Golden

Chakra: #2 Sacral Chakra (Svadisthana)

Element: Fire

Magical Uses: Naturally purifies the spirit and the mind. Amazing ability to draw disease and pain away from the body, physically, mentally, and spiritually through the absorption of stagnant or negative energies and transform them into positive and clear energy. Unblocks the sacral and navel chakras. I use it as part of my cleansing rituals or when I cast healing spells. I put it on top of the photo of the person for whom I desire healing magic.

3. AMETHYST

Colors: Purple, violet, dark purple

Chakra: #6 Third Eye Chakra (Ajna)

Element: Air

Magical Uses: Boosts the immune system, improves endocrine function, enhances the skin's appearance, promotes a healthy digestive system, alleviates headaches, balances hormones, reduces stress and anxiety, promotes cleansing, cures insomnia.

4. AQUAMARINE

Colors: Blue, greenish blue, dark blue

Chakra: #5 Throat Chakra (Vishudha)

Element: Water

Magical Uses: Releases creativity and wisdom. Provides increased fortitude due to its calming effect. Promotes harmony in relationships as it inspires tolerance and compromise. Strengthens fidelity and commitment like the waters that flow upon the Earth. Protection crystal while at sea or with any water-related activity. Promotes allergy healing and a healthy immune system, pituitary gland, and liver.

5. AZURITE

Color: Deep blue

Chakra: #6 Third Eye Chakra (Ajna)

Element: Water

Magical Uses: Emotionally healing vibrational energy. Strengthens and cleans the emotional body, letting go of worry and stress. Provides an acceptance and understanding of irrational fears and where they came from. Used for spinal alignments and vertebral disorders, pain related to malformed rib-cage development and small bones, and healing properties for arthritis and joint problems.

6. BLACK KYANITE

Colors: Black, orange, green, indigo, yellow, rare white, pink, gray

Chakra: #1 Root Chakra (Muladhara)

Element: Water

Magical Uses: Manifesting intentions, promotes psychic abilities, healing energy, effective communication, strengthens relationships, balances root chakra. Place it between your feet on the floor for grounding energy. It is my favorite grounding crystal. Carries very high vibrations while offering protection and opens the earth star chakra.

- The earth star chakra is a more recently discovered chakra situated under your feet (not part of the physical body) and is directly connected to the Earth's core. It grounds the entire chakra system.

7. BLACK OBSIDIAN

Color: Black

Chakra: #1 Root Chakra (Muladhara)

Element: Water

Magical Uses: Extremely powerful crystal for protection. Helps you examine and recognize your dark side (we all have a dark side) and clears it from your psyche. It does not hide from dark energies; instead, it shines a light on the darkness and negativity and strips it from your path, leading you toward love and light. While often utilized for protection, the black obsidian crystal has amazing healing properties for grief and loss, as well as broken heartedness and other emotional struggles.

8. BLUE CALCITE

Colors: Blue, clear, whitish, pale (*blue* is special)

Chakra: #5 Throat Chakra (Vishudha)

Element: Water

Magical Uses: Is there a speaker in the house? Blue calcite takes away any shyness and helps you to articulate your words, even when you are communicating electronically, even when you're texting. Communication is still energy and energy doesn't discriminate. It is soothing to the nervous system and helps alleviate anxiety. It connects the intellectual mind to the emotional mind and balances them, giving way to better health and wellness. Physically it keeps your bones and teeth strong due to its relationship with calcium.

9. BLOODSTONE

Colors: Red, green

Chakra: #1 Root Chakra (Muladhara) and #4 Heart Chakra (Anahata)

Element: Fire

Magical Uses: Grounding, decision making, protection, courage, friendships, idealism, unselfishness, spiritual harmony, intense healing. Boosts the immune system, purifies blood, kidneys, liver, spleen, bladder, eliminates toxins, aids in circulation, in blood disorders such as anemia, and heals infections. This is a very important crystal to use on a regular basis. There are numerous scholarly articles on the benefits and healing properties of bloodstone crystals. Women have been using them for centuries to prevent miscarriages and to give themselves strength during labor and childbirth. The bloodstone has an amazing ability to alleviate problems associated with PMS and menopause.

10. CELESTITE

Colors: Gray, green, orange, yellow, brown, blue

Chakra: #6 Third Eye Chakra (Ajna)

Element: Spirit

Magical Uses: Healing eyes, nasal, ears, digestion, mental illness. Removes toxins from the bloodstream, alleviates pain, brings good luck, balance, peace, truth, and enlightenment. Restores chakra balance, provides purification of the chakra, inner wisdom, helps you to remember your dreams. The thing I love most about this crystal is that it really helps me spiritually. When I place it on the third eye chakra, I get a sense of levitation and divine love! It balances my yin and yang energies.

11. CLEAR QUARTZ

Color: Translucent

Chakra: #7 Crown Chakra (Sahasrara)

Element: Spirit

Magical Uses: Master of all healers, boosts the immune system, amps up physical, emotional, and spiritual energies, powers up your intention, acts as pain relief, and promotes positivity. The clear quartz crystal enhances people's auras. I have seen it with my own eyes! I use it to keep my whole body in check. It opens, cleanses, unblocks, and activates all chakras. Keep it close by if you are studying, as it strongly influences concentration.

12. CITRINE

Color: Yellowish

Chakra: #3 Navel Chakra (Solar Plexus Chakra) (Manipura), all of the chakras

Element: Fire

Magical Uses: Self-discipline, prosperity, chakra cleanser, harmony within the family, healing agent for digestive, bowel, and spine problems. It is also an energy enhancer, weight loss help, optimism promoter, and CFS (chronic fatigue syndrome) healer. Cupping the crystal each day and stating your goals aloud to the universe will ramp up its energy tenfold. Citrine works with your root chakra and helps you to realize your dreams. It is an energy provider. That is why it helps those who are suffering from fatigue. But, if you think about it, with increased energy comes professional growth. I use it the same way I take my vitamin C.

13. FLUORITE

Colors: Purple, clear, green, blue, rare yellow, rainbow

Chakra: Purple- #6 Third Eye Chakra (Ajna); Blue- #7 Crown Chakra (Sahasrara); Green- #4 Heart Chakra (Anahata); Yellow- #3 Navel Chakra (Manipura); Rainbow- all chakras.

Element: Air and Water

Magical Uses: Detoxes the mind! Blue fluorite: the crystal of singers. Calm, spirituality, clarity, and logical thinking. Green fluorite: helps with addictions, cleansing, and creativity. Purple fluorite increases self-confidence, improves coordination and balance, and concentration. Rainbow fluorite helps with nervous system irregularities, promotes accurate fortune telling (runes, tarot, etc.), and has anti-viral properties. Yellow fluorite is a liver healing crystal that also lowers cholesterol and removes toxins.

14. GARNET

Colors: Dark red, green or olive, dark yellow, black

Chakra: #4 Heart Chakra (Anahata)

Element: Fire

Magical Uses: Honesty, sincerity, libido, self-confidence. It also keeps you steady on your feet during crisis intervention and improves your courage. Garnet aids in blood disorders and improves circulation. Something about Garnet makes me feel very safe. Passions are ignited with garnet!

15. GREEN AVENTURINE

Color: Green

Chakra: #4 Heart Chakra (Anahata)

Element: Earth

Magical Uses: Money and wealth. Transforms negative energy into positive energy. Protects your home and garden from electromagnetic pollution. Promotes compassion and self-confidence. This crystal protects you from heartbreak, and in later years, if you desire, will attract a love interest of great potential. Gives you the power to embrace change and fills you with an understanding of true acceptance.

16. GREEN JADE

Color: Green

Chakra: #4 Heart Chakra (Anahata)

Element: Earth

Magical Uses: Money. Inspires devotion, loyalty, love, protects against misfortune and accidents. Helps with disorders of the kidney and heart and helps with anxiety. Whenever I am involved with green jade, I always seem to be able to vividly remember my dreams. It enhances clarity, wisdom, emotional balance, and inner peace.

17. HEMATITE

Colors: Black, gray, red, brown; all have a distinguishing characteristic of a reddish-brown streak.

Chakra: #1 Root Chakra (Muladhara)

Element: Fire

Magical Uses: Stress reduction. Grounding and protection. Pulls in positive vibrational energy. Brings harmony to the mind, body, and spirit. Helps with legalities. Brings money, aids in decision-making, works for manifestation, focus, clarity, stability, protection, balance, divination, problem-solving, emotions, doubt, anxiety, communication, and strength.

18. LAPIS LAZULI

Color: Deep blue

Chakra: #5 Throat Chakra (Vishudha) and #6 Third Eye Chakra (Ajna)

Element: Water

Magical Uses: Wards off evil. Improves eyesight. Alleviates headaches, skin problems, anxiety, and stress. Protection, self-expression, truthfulness, and moral compass. Stimulates clarity, objectivity, and creativity. Reveals your inner-most truths. It really helps new relationships to bond and allows for freedom of expression.

19. LEPIDOLITE

Colors: Lilac and rose-violet

Chakra: #4 Heart Chakra (Anahata), #6 Third Eye Chakra (Ajna) and #7 Crown Chakra (Sahasrara)

Element: Water

Magical Uses: Meditation, transition, awareness, and emotional balance. It rids the mind and body of negativity, opens the heart, throat, and third eye chakras, aids in overcoming addiction and provides a much-needed boost to the immune system for everyone, but most importantly for addicts. I have an ol' friend who swears by Lepidolite for treating his sciatica and diabetic neuropathy! It is a stress reliever and helps anxiety. A number of articles on the Internet discussed the use of Lepidolite for treating bipolar disorder.

20. ORANGE AVENTURINE

Color: Orange

Chakra: #2 Sacral Chakra (Svadisthana)

Element: Water

Magical Uses: Promotes normal sexual functioning. Enhances creativity and spiritual growth. Helps with problem-solving and decision-making. Helps you to be mindful of the present moment and how you are feeling right now. Enhances feelings of contentment, joy, happiness, and positivity. This crystal does an amazing job at relaxing me and allowing me to notice the simple pleasures in life. It also helps individuals suffering from PTSD.

21. ROSE QUARTZ

Color: Pink

Chakra: #4 Heart Chakra (Anahata) and #5 Throat Chakra (Vishudha)

Element: Water

Magical Uses: Heals the heart and soul. Prevents heart attacks and thrombosis. Improves circulation and keeps your heart muscles strong and running smoothly. Protection during pregnancy for both unborn child and mother. Promotes the flow of unconditional love and unbreakable bonds. It is the heart stone. Because of its relationship with the heart, rose quartz crystals also attract romantic love interests. It heals the pain of deep emotional trauma and improves self-worth. Carries the warmth of motherhood and teaches you how to soothe the self; to heal yourself with your own hands.

22. MOONSTONE

Colors: Opalescent, milky whites with variants of blue, gray, pink or green

Chakra: #3 Navel Chakra (Solar Plexus Chakra) (Manipura)

Element: Water

Magical Uses: Helps with reproduction, childbirth, and hormonal issues and breastfeeding. Balance, self-care, stress relief, insight, healing, and work productivity. Eliminates excess body fluids and toxins, aids in digestion, and nourishes fleshy organs such as your pancreas and liver. Helps men and women to be more open to their emotional selves. I read a lot of articles that referred to moonstone helping men open up to their emotions. However, my experience is that it makes me more receptive to my emotions, too.

23. OPAL

Colors: Nearly all colors (rainbow hues). It is a magnificent play of color energies used to vitalize chakras that correspond with each other and then link them to the crown chakra.

Chakra: #7 Crown Chakra (Sahasrara)

Element: Air and Water

Magical Uses: Brings alive your mystical and psychic characteristics, while advancing your cosmic intuition and consciousness. It raises your insight, allowing you to journey deep into self-healing or regress into past lives. It is a protector and can be used as a shamanic guide. It is my primary grounding crystal because of its magnificent way of helping me to invoke visions. It is physically beneficial for the health of hair, nails, eyes, and skin.

24. RUBY

Color: Pure red

Chakra: #1 Root Chakra (Muladhara)

Element: Fire

Magical Uses: The queen of crystals and an aphrodisiac! Helps with fatigue and lethargy, Stimulates energy and circulation of the entire body. It can be overly stimulating for some, yet also calming to those who are hyperactive. If you are planning on entering a debate, make sure to sport a ruby somewhere on your person. It fights exhaustion and lethargy.

25. SAPPHIRE

Colors: Blue, yellow, black, pink, white, indigo, green

Chakra: Black- #1 Root Chakra (Muladhara); Blue- #5 Throat Chakra (Vishudha); Green- #4 Heart Chakra (Anahata); Indigo- #6 Third Eye Chakra (Ajna); Pink- #4 Heart Chakra (Anahata); White- #7 Crown Chakra (Sahasrara); Yellow- #3 Navel/Solar Plexus Chakra (Manipura)

Element: Water

Magical Uses: All sapphires have the following qualities, but some are stronger with specific colors: grounding, memory, good luck and wisdom, intuition, attraction, generosity, spirituality, increased self-worth, loyalty, and independence. Works to combat blood and circulatory disorders, throat problems, and nerve disorders.

26. SUGILITE

Color: Violet

Chakra: #7 Crown Chakra (Sahasrara)

Element: Spirit

Magical Uses: Awakens the crown chakra and permeates light throughout your body. Encourages acceptance, forgiveness, and hope. Stress reduction; it also instills confidence and increases self-esteem. Provides a greater awareness of the mind-body connection. Brings light to the darkness and combats fears and anxieties. Opens the third eye chakra and helps you to recover your dreams and makes them rich in meaning and significance. Relieves headaches. Also, a grounding force. Removes negative karma. Inspires awe!

27. SUN STONE

Colors: Gold, orange, red and brown

Chakra: #2 Sacral Chakra (Svadisthana)

Element: Fire

Magical Uses: The abundance crystal encourages originality and independence. This one can make you rich and famous. It is a good luck charm when participating in any competition. It will inspire you to reveal your talents and do so without fear! Brings about great enthusiasm and will make a fitness program seem appealing. If your job requires labor or long hours, you can count on a sun stone in your pocket to give you the energy you need to succeed. In the workplace, it is nice to keep one on your desk, as it will enhance your profile and bring you new opportunities for advancement and leadership. Keep one next to your computer, especially if you have an online business. It will also protect you from any beings that are emotionally draining as it is a stress reducer by nature. It shines light on dark places with its brilliance, so it helps those with phobias or fear of the dark.

28. TIGER'S EYE

Color: Golden to red brown

Chakra: #1 Root Chakra (Muladhara), #2 Sacral Chakra (Svadhisthana), and Navel Chakra (Manipura)

Element: Fire and Earth

Magical Uses: Brings good luck, promotes clarity, problem-solving, improves focus, balances yin and yang, and is a mood stabilizer. Enhances purpose, courage, willpower, self-worth; reduces stress and tension. Heightened awareness, optimism, sheds light on situations, helping you to see things more clearly. Inspiration, grounding, empowerment, helps you to look at things logically. Enhances libido. Aids in reducing fatigue by providing positive energy.

29. TURQUOISE

Color: Blue

Chakra: #5 Throat Chakra (Vishudha)

Element: Air

Magical Uses: Helps to heal any areas associated with the throat, ears, nose, and lungs. Alleviates allergies, headaches, asthma, and any other bronchial problems due to its cool and soothing properties. Calms panic attacks and is great for grounding. It is one of the oldest crystals known to man. It strengthens your immune system and rebalances the mind, soul, and body. I love it because it really helps to clear up my thinking when I feel overwhelmed.

30. ZEBRA JASPER

Colors: White with black stripes, green, red, and brown with white

Chakra: #1 Root Chakra (Muladhara)

Element: Fire

Magical Uses: Balances and unites feminine and masculine energies and your chakras. Encourages optimism, even when under stressful conditions. Inspires you to turn your dreams into reality. Helps with muscle pain, kidney and bladder issues, skin conditions, and strengthens your teeth and bones. Grounding properties. I always feel very connected to Mother Earth when I use this crystal. When I do that successfully, I am filled with joy!

5

PREPARATION

When it comes to preparing for spell casting, there is much to do in order for your manifestations to be successful. You can think about casting a spell in the same manner as you would follow a recipe for your favorite dish. You know you want it to come out right! Knowing how to prepare to cast your spells is every bit as important as how you cast your spell. As you know by now, the clarity of your INTENTION is the most important thing. You don't have to build an altar to do a spell, but it will make your magic more organized and will provide you with a sacred space for you to focus your energy and intention. It can also be a beautiful place for you to turn to when you want to feel good about yourself and the universe.

Start out by finding a beautiful and meaningful piece of material. Your altar cloth can be green if your intention is abundance, for example. You can build your altar wherever you choose. I have mine on a table in the corner of my bedroom facing east to catch the rising sun. Years ago, I started out with one on my dresser and then on my coffee table. Finally, I wanted a place that could be devoted to my altar, so I bought a handcrafted wooden spell table with the tree of life etched on it. It's beautiful. There are many to choose from online starting at around $35. Every item selected for your altar should be something to which you feel spiritually and personally connected. Every witch's journey is unique, so make use of items from which you feel a positive emotional vibration or energy.

Preparing Your Altar

Choosing the color of your cloth (make sure you use cloth you are drawn to and that feels good on your skin) depends on what you want to achieve:

- Red (fire element): Love, courage, passion, power, professional goals, and creativity.
- Orange (fire element): Attraction, success, property, and justice.
- Yellow (air element): Happiness, learning, memory, and intelligence.
- Green (earth element): Abundance, money, fertility, nature, health, and personal growth.
- Blue (water element): Serenity, spirituality, patience, wisdom, psychic abilities, and protection.

- Purple (water element): Power, psychic abilities, ambition, acceptance, and royalty.
- Pink (fire element): Friendship, romance, health and well-being, love, and nurturing.
- White (air element): Cleansing, peace, and purity, confidence, clarity, and inspiration.
- Silver (water element): Dreams, astral projections, intuition, telepathy, communication, and positivity.
- Gold (fire element): Success, happiness, prosperity, luck, wealth, attention, enlightenment, and popularity.
- Brown (earth element): Animals, favors, family, health, friendships, grounding, strength, and balance.

If you give glory to a deity, include symbols referencing them and their magic. Trust your intuition when placing items on your altar. Usually, at least four candles are placed on the altar to connect it to north, south, east, and west. Items representing each of the elements are also used. I have a gorgeous crystal bowl filled with blessed water and small floating candles in it, and at the bottom I have a tiny moonstone crystal. I am honoring water on the western side of my altar. You can use any symbols you want, but here are some suggestions:

- East (air) — feather, wand, knife, magnifying glass, wing
- West (water) — goblet, river stones, bowl of water, seashells, salt

- South (fire) — yellow flowers, orange or red crystals, matches
- North (earth) — bones, plant, rocks, bonsai

How to Cleanse Your Altar

It is essential to cleanse your altar on a regular basis because it rids the room of unwanted or negative energies and allows space for beneficial and positive energies. Just like cleaning our homes, we should clean our altars. Negative energies can come to the altar by way of items or people coming into and leaving the room. Cleansing your altar imbues it with respect. To charge your altar means to fill the area with your energy and intentions or with an element's or deity's intentions. Charging your altar is also important to your magical process. Here is how I charge and cleanse my altar. You can tailor or change it to fit your preferences or needs.

Necessary items:

- Sage or other smudge item or incense (and something to light it with).
- Fireproof plate or abalone shell (to hold under your smudge bundle); you can use an incense holder.
- Witch hazel, holy water, or lemon juice and a clean cloth.

Steps for cleansing:

1. Remove everything from the altar and put to the side.

2. Wipe down the entire altar in a counterclockwise motion. The whole time you are cleansing, speak aloud "begone negative energies from my altar." Clean it thoroughly so that it is acceptable to you for communicating with divine energy.

3. Continuing with your intentions, clean all of the items, tools, or any other magical supplies before placing them on the altar.

4. Light your smudge bundle and wave its smoke in a counterclockwise direction all around your altar. While waving the smoke, imagine it evaporating all negative vibrations. Then do the same for all of your items.

Charging Your Crystals

In order to successfully improve and change your life for the better using crystals, you have to be dedicated to their cleansing and charging on a regular basis. The positive vibrational energies given by crystals require upkeep and attention. With charging comes added energy, enhancing your crystal's vibrancy and magical longevity before it has to be cleansed again. Also, charging your crystal can raise its intensity and the intensity of any spell placed into it.

Moonlight Charging

Moonlight charges your crystals with a gentle and soft feminine energy and works well as a facilitator for change, like switching jobs, moving to a new home, or a relationship breakup. It also works well in providing you clarity and introspection.

1. For sunlight and moonlight charging, lay your crystals out either in a grid or pattern, according to your intuition, so that they receive direct moonlight or sunlight. If you can, expose your crystals for 24 hours so they can get the most energy from both. Full moons symbolize new beginnings. Energies differ according to the phases of the moon, which offers feminine energies:

- Full moon: waning energy.
- The new moon: growth energy.

Sunlight Charging

1. The following is a list of crystals that will not fade in the sun and work best with the sun-powered energy:
2. Obsidian: it is commonly found in its original state outdoors; it is volcanic and will not fade.
3. Clear quartz: because there is no pigmentation in this crystal, it does well in direct sunlight for charging, but be careful it does not ignite sparks and starts a fire.

4. Tourmaline: this is a fantastic grounding crystal that is safe to charge in sunlight.

5. Moonstone: this crystal is perfect for charging under the moon and the sun, so its feminine and masculine energies become balanced.

6. Charging your crystals in indirect sunlight is good for those prone to fading or becoming brittle if exposed to direct sunlight. Pick a nice shady spot in your yard, garden or windowsill that faces a sun-filled area but is not quite reachable to the sun. You can also cup your crystal and meditate outside for 15 minutes or so. If all else fails, place your crystals under a representative of the sun such as a glowing candle. Do it in a room that is dark so the candle can shine brightly.

Earth Charging

You can either place your crystal directly into the earth and bury it or you can put it in a box or a jar to retrieve later. Charge your crystals this way for at least seven hours. Call the earth and soil back to your stones for charging. This is a natural charging method that allows your crystals to reprogram their connection to the Earth so they can renew their powerful healing energies. Crystals that work best with this method are:

- Agate
- Boji stone
- Calcite

- Carnelian
- Jasper
- Mahogany
- Obsidian

Setting the Intention of the Crystal

It is imperative that you communicate exactly what support you want and where you want it from your crystals. Your intentions may change over time. Intention setting is a powerful and helpful exercise in crystal magic and can bring you more joy, positivity, happiness, balance, abundance, and all-around good vibrations. Whatever your intended goals may be, they all start with an intention, and your crystals are the tools to use to set you on your journey of manifesting your personal dreams and objectives. Crystals have tremendous power to bring your intentions to fruition. They serve as a visual aid to remind you of your objectives in life and can be a useful physical tool for setting your intentions routinely. If setting your intention to your crystals is a new practice, here is an easy step-by-step technique.

Note that you can always change your ritual to compliment your gut feelings; the more you make it yours the more powerful your magic:

1. Cleanse and connect: You will be drawn to varying crystals for different reasons. Maybe one day, a certain

color makes you resonate with a specific crystal. Or maybe you looked up the properties of a certain crystal to meet a certain need or power you want to harness. Trusting your intuition is the most important part of connecting and then going with the crystal(s) you are drawn to.

2. Once you have chosen the crystal(s) you want to set your intentions to, use the previous methods to clean and charge them.

3. Clear your mind of all negativity and take several deep breaths or meditate for a few moments with your crystal.

4. Choose your intention that fits your objectives, something you need rather than want.

5. Keeping a still mind, focus on your intention and your crystal.

6. Write your intention on a piece of paper while maintaining your focus on your connection to your crystal.

7. Speak aloud your intention to your crystal while holding it over your third eye.

8. Continue the process until your mind and body feel that your intention is set.

9. After setting your intention, keep your crystal close to keep your objectives at the forefront of your brain. You can place it under your pillow and sleep on it. It is best if you can see it, though, such as on your desk. I keep

my clear quartz and green tourmaline on a small glass plate. This was the glass top to one of my candles and now it is a perfect little vessel for my crystals to sit on while I am writing or networking on my computer.

10. Say thank you! Whenever doing magic, it is important to express your appreciation to the spirits for your blessings. It is also a beautiful way to end your rituals. You can do this with a quick gratitude list where you write down three things you are grateful for or make an offering to a deity of your choice; whichever fits your personal beliefs.

11. Reset and revisit your intentions to help you as you continue on your unique spiritual journey. You may choose to set your rituals for each full or new moon, thereby making it a monthly ritual.

How to Store Your Crystals

You can keep from chipping your crystals if you store them in individual containers or pouches. Many spiritual advisors recommend only using natural materials, so they stay free from negative or outside energy. But I found that natural materials actually work as conductors of energy, so I keep my small crystals in small plastic boxes to steer clear of outside influences. I keep them in a daily medicine container because they have divided compartments. I also put a piece of tissue underneath so that the crystal is resting on a soft bed. Do your best not to store hard crystals with very soft ones, so as to avoid scratching or nicking the soft crystals. Calcite and fluorite crystals break easily, so use caution when storing hard stones. If you want them to be displayed while stored, keep them away from direct sunlight and any extreme changes in temperature.

Take the time to look up crystals in your collection for helpful hints on what can potentially damage them. For example, lodestone and hematite oxidize or they can rust if left out in the open air. Some crystals, such as selenite, dissolve in hot water. Moldavite fractures in hot water. For these reasons, I emphasize the importance of doing your homework. Check out the Mohs scale of mineral hardness. It tells you how easily crystals scratch, with 1 being very soft and 10 being the hardest (which is a diamond). It is a good guide to use to tell you if you can carry your crystal safely in your pocket or if it should be in a velvet pouch. In general, if your crystal has a rating of 6 or higher on the Mohs scale, you can safely clean it in water.

6

CRYSTAL GRIDS

When our most precious crystals are combined with a bit of geometry for the specific intention of manifesting our deepest desires, goals, dreams, and objectives, we have a crystal grid. If you think about it, geometry is sacred and it is everywhere, it is in our architecture, the branches and leaves of the trees, the galaxies and their spirals, and the cells in our bodies. By studying geometry we can better understand the world around us and unlock the mysteries of creation. When placed under a microscope, crystals reveal that they are made up of a perfect crystalline foundation that show patterns that repeat themselves in perfect geometrical form. So, by making crystal grids, you are aligning your intentions with the right crystals and their geometric form necessary to manifest your objectives.

Select at least four crystals to start your grid, keeping your intention in mind. You can use all of the same type or combine types, again depending on your intention. It's best to place the biggest one in the middle. Once you have decided on your crystals, gather them together and cleanse and charge them using any of the techniques previously discussed. Once you have performed your cleansing and charging ritual, consider your combinations. Here are some suggestions for enhancing your grid:

- For banishing: onyx, obsidian, hematite, and jade.
- For healing: agate, amethyst, jasper, tourmaline, rose quartz, or stones representing your chakras.
- For personal growth: sunstone, clear quartz, and carnelian.

Forming your Crystal Grid Pattern

Decide on a geometric pattern. This can be a pentacle, circle, spiral or any of a thousand others out there. Pick one that you feel connected to. You can even use a deity as a template. Some geometric patterns lend themselves to healing, abundance, protection, and well-being. One of my favorite patterns for my most recent crystal grid is a part of the flower of life (the basic spatial pattern of our universe), namely, the seed of life, because it symbolizes all possible beginnings and all possible journeys, a path to infinite possibilities.

Here are instructions on how to draw the seed of life pattern.

1. Start by using a compass to draw a circle.
2. Draw another circle anywhere along the circle you just drew.

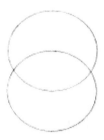

1. Place the tip of the compass at the intersecting points of the circles and draw two more circles. Repeat the process until you have six circles.
2. Put the tip of the compass where the black dot is below and draw the 7th circle.

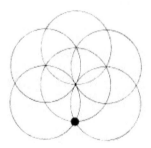

1. These 7 circles comprise what is known as the Seed of Life.

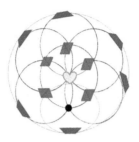

There aren't any fast rules or rules set in stone when it comes to constructing your crystal grids; it always goes back to working with how you feel the crystals are guiding you; your intuition. There are many tutorials on how to best make them. For me personally, I think the most powerful manifesting comes from your own intuition. Some like to use their crystal grid as part of a more complex ritual. You may also want to keep it very simple. Other shapes include:

- The egg of life is the addition of six more circles to your seed of life, symbolizing fertility, life, and rebirth.
- The flower of life is composed of 19 circles and is thought to be the basic structure of the universe; every atom, every molecule, and every life form.
- The tree of life is our connection to everything unseen. It is a reminder that you are not alone but part of an interconnected universe. It shows a hierarchical

formation for all of the universe's forces and is made up of 10 spheres (Sephiroth). Beginning at the top, the first sphere symbolizes cosmic consciousness, and the sphere at the bottom symbolizes the material world. The spheres in between symbolize different aspects of the soul.

- The fruit of life is the holiest of the sacred geometry because it is hidden within the pattern of the flower of life. It has 13 spheres, representing the transition and unity between dimensions/worlds. Think about the keys on a piano; the thirteenth note is actually a higher frequency of the first note.

- Metatron's cube is the culmination of the centers of the 13 spheres connecting into 78 lines. This sacred geometrical structure has all of the above-mentioned patterns and every possible law of geometry, making up what we experience as physical reality.

Where to Place your Crystal Grid

You can place it on a cloth or paper with sacred geometry drawn on it, or you can put leaves or flowers within your grid. What you place underneath your grid is unique to your liking; you can use living energy such as bamboo or other types of wood, or you can use a mirror or glass to spread your crystal's energy. You can put your grid right on the ground and feel connected to Mother Earth's field of energy. Since crystal grids serve as a reminder of your intentions, every time you see it, your mind can focus. For this reason, it is nice to have it on display. I don't think there is a specific room in which to place your crystal grid, but it could be that your space is limited. If you meditate on it, some ideas may come to mind. For instance, if your intention is prosperity, you may have it in your office. If your intention is protection, you may want your crystal grid by the front or back door. Of course, if you have created it for better sleep, well, I guess you know where it goes! However, I highly suggest putting some space between your crystal grid and your bed or where you sleep (don't put it under your bed) because their strong energy fields can cause a sleep disturbance. You can always test it out yourself, but if you are limited in space, and have the crystal grid near your sleeping area, only put it there when you don't have to get up early.

Setting up your Grid

As I said earlier, when designing your crystal grid, using your intuition is the best method to follow. However, usually crystal grids have crystals (called Way Stones) surrounding a center stone. Crystals that amplify the other crystals are also important. Crystals have "auras" just like all living things. People have their chakra line to center them. When you design a crystal grid, the center crystal is the grid's anchor, which behaves as an antenna to let the universe and spiritual realm know your intentions. The central crystal is commonly the largest stone with the highest vibrational energy. The crystals surrounding the center stone are the ones geometrically arranged. The number of surrounding crystals depends on how complex or simple you want to make your grid, and the shape you have decided upon. These surrounding crystals are the great grid communicators, broadcasting and receiving your intention out into the universe like satellites. If you have formatted your crystals in a square or wheel pattern, create a spoke-type energy pattern by moving your finger from the surrounding crystals to the center crystal.

If you want to make a more complex grid, tumbles or quartz points typically function as *amplification stones*. They are optional, but they do amp up the grid even more. The amplification stones are placed geometrically between the surrounding crystals. You can also place an item, referred to as an object of importance, on your grid. Some examples include a photo of a special person in our life, flowers, a letter, jewelry, leaves, or any other important object aligned with your intention. If you use the keyword 'crystal grid' and click on images in your search engine of choice, you will see hundreds, if not thousands of examples. Choose carefully where this grid will be set up and take into consideration how much time will be needed for the grid to manifest its purpose.

Activating your Grid

At this point, either with your hands, a favorite crystal, or a metal wand, extend your field of energy to transmit and magnify your intention into the grid. Prior to activation, conjure up a concise announcement of what you plan to manifest. While waving your wand, pendulum, crystal, or hands, speak aloud your intention to the center crystal. Imagine it beginning to glow with your intention and the heightened energy being produced. Then, with your hand or wand hovering above each crystal and moving in a counterclockwise motion, connecting the crystals, visualize the aura surrounding the grid. When you think the time is right, end with an expression of gratitude for the support and encouragement of your crystals. To increase or stimulate your crystal grid's energy, imagine connecting lines that link each individual crystal's energy, making one cohesive unit. If you bump crystals out of place, you will need to reactivate the grid. With your intention set to linking all of the crystals' energy, starting at the center, use your wand or smudge bundle and make a line connecting to a crystal on the outside of the grid. Then in a clockwise fashion make a line to the next crystal and then back to the center crystal again. Go back over the same line and move clockwise to the next surrounding crystal and then back to the center crystal again. Once you have outlined the surrounding crystals, if you have amplifying crystals in the grid, make a line with your wand, finger, or smudge bundle to include them. Make sure to end up with your point toward the center crystal to charge it with universal energy so that it may manifest your objective. Keep in mind that crystals are magical on their own, but when combined with your intention and intuition, their power is unstoppable.

7

CRYSTAL ELIXIRS

E ssential oils are soothing to the mind, the soul, and the body. Essential oils combined with the healing and magical powers of crystals will promote your health and wellness, as well as clearing, unblocking, and balancing your chakras. Crystals and essential oils work synergistically to enhance your intention, and the energy you want to manifest. In case you are wondering what the two have in common, well, both are made from natural resources in the earth and both are used for magic and healing purposes. Crystals naturally occur as minerals in the earth and are discovered all over the globe. Essential oils are directly distilled from trees, plants, and flowers. I have been experimenting with essential oil and crystal pairings for quite some time now, and I have come to realize that when the crystal and oil have a similar vibrational energy, they enhance each other's ways of guiding you toward the state of being that you want to achieve. To do this, get a small crystal that will fit into a small essential oil glass container. Place the crystal in the bottle and fill the container ¾ of the way with the essential oil.

The following is a list of pairings between crystals and essential oils and their magical uses:

AMETHYST: Pairs with cypress, sandalwood, and frankincense.
Magical use: Provides balance, protection, and self-confidence.

AMAZONITE: Pairs with orange, bergamot, clove, juniper, geranium, and spruce.
Magical use: Provides truth and courage, dispels worry, negative energy, and fear.

APATITE: Pairs with orange, nutmeg, peppermint, and grapefruit.
Magical use: Stimulates growth, motivation, goal setting, energy.

AQUAMARINE: Pairs with ginger, lavender, helichrysum, clove, and chamomile.
Magical use: Enhances self-expression, helpful for closure, relaxes the mind.

BLUE CALCITE: Pairs with geranium, basil, frankincense, vetiver, and lavender.
Magical use: Facilitates communication and is considered the crystal of trust.

CITRINE: Pairs with ginger, orange, patchouli, sandalwood and clove.
Magical use: Creativity, success, power, and abundance.

CHRYSOCOLLA: Pairs with ylang ylang, helichrysum, tangerine, sandalwood, basil, and lavender.
Magical use: Teaching crystal, encourages peace, compassion, and forgiveness.

CLEAR QUARTZ: Pairs with all essential oils.
Magical use: Amps up any intent or energy that is invested into it.

EMERALD: Pairs with cedarwood, jasmine, rose, patchouli, and lavender.
Magical use: Promotes unity and friendship, relaxing effect, encourages positivity.

EMERALD CALCITE: Pairs with ylang ylang, clue tansy, tangerine, and patchouli.
Magical use: Crystal of peace, supportive during any transitions in life.

GARNET: Pairs with jasmine, lemon, ylang ylang, frankincense, and orange.

Magical use: Positive crystal, inspires devotion and love, antidepressant.

HERKIMER DIAMOND: Pairs with sage, tea tree, clove, lemon, and frankincense.

Magical use: Promotes self-appreciation and works as a healing agent; emotional, spiritual, and physical.

LABRADORITE: Pairs with peppermint, neroli, basil, and lemon.

Magical use: Inspiration, clarity, lets you envision many possibilities all at the same time.

LAPIS LAZULI: Pairs with spruce, lime, basil, jasmine, and frankincense.

Magical use: Inspires knowledge and good judgment, creates a desire for the truth and wisdom; considered a stone of truth.

ORANGE KYANITE: Pairs with grapefruit, jasmine, orange, lavender, and geranium.

Magical use: Encourages optimism, playfulness, enhances self-esteem.

PERIDOT: Pairs with cypress, jasmine, cinnamon, patchouli, and bergamot.

Magical use: Helps to overcome resentment and fear, assisting you to move forward with your life, manifests prosperity and abundance.

PINK LEMURIAN (quartz): Pairs with sage, ylang ylang, lavender, and bergamot.

Magical use: Feminine energy, love, heightened spirituality, meditation, unconditional love; attracts angels into your life.

PINK OPAL: Pairs with orange, sandalwood, juniper and frankincense.

Magical use: Crystal of renewal, balances your emotions, calming effect.

PYRITE: Pairs with grapefruit, clove, peppermint, and frankincense.

Magical use: Promotes leadership, energizes creativity, and acts as a protective agent.

RAINBOW MOONSTONE: Pairs with bergamot, cypress, rose, vetiver, and lavender.

Magical use: Calming crystal, helps during change by providing insight.

RHODOLITE (a variety of Garnet): Pairs with cedarwood, coriander, rosemary, spruce, and tangerine.
Magical use: A warming crystal that inspires your intuition and promotes contemplation.

ROSE QUARTZ: Pairs with bergamot, lavender, ylang ylang, rose, and jasmine.
Magical use: The crystal of love and relationships.

RUBY: Pairs with cinnamon, rose, ginger, peppermint, and ylang ylang.
Magical uses: Makes you motivated and able to concentrate. Gives you energy; associated with love.

SAPPHIRE: Pairs with orange, vetiver, lavender, bergamot, and ylang ylang.
Magical use: Brings joy, commitment and love, balances chakras.

SUNSTONE: Pairs with myrrh, frankincense, clove, and orange.
Magical use: Inspires self-nurturing and is considered the crystal of joy.

TANGERINE QUARTZ: Pairs with fir, chamomile, tangerine, patchouli, and frankincense.

Magical use: Grounding crystal that allows you to leave the past behind, boosts creativity, and is soothing.

TANZANITE: Pairs with rose, sandalwood, chamomile, frankincense, and geranium.
Magical use: Meditation crystal, connects your heart and mind, enhances communication.

TOPAZ: Pairs with bergamot, orange, jasmine, rosemary, and sandalwood.
Magical use: Crystal of good fortune, enhances confidence, prompts joyfulness and goal attainment.

TOURMALINE: Pairs with myrrh, geranium, orange, bergamot, hyssop, and fir.
Magical use: Enhances self-awareness; an inspirational crystal that promotes compassion and understanding.

TURQUOISE: Pairs with fennel, rosemary, clove, Palo Santo, cypress, and frankincense.
Magical use: Calming crystal, protection, and creativity.

II

THE SPELLS

Crystals, obviously, are beautiful to look at and full of positive energy. They are the fastest way to make your space magic. But the most powerful way to use your crystals is by using them in your magic. Whether it is for love or healing, abundance or success, you can harness their natural energy for many of your mystical endeavors. Part Two will fill your enquiring mind with spells from A to Z.

8

HEALING SPELLS

Crystals, inherently, vary in their energies and professed healing properties. To harness their energy, you must program your crystals with a specific intention. As you continue to practice with one stone, you will have an even deeper connection with your intention. The crystal's magic amplifies your intentions, and the two together make a powerful healing tool. By using your clear and specific intention, you can program your crystals and manifest your desire in healing.

Grief and Loss Spell Jar

Dealing with loss is far from easy but grief can feel all-consuming. There are many painful types of loss, such as losing a loved one, losing a job, or even our years as they pass by. There is no straight path through grief, but there are techniques to help you ease or shift the overwhelming energy that is the product of loss. Your crystals can't wipe away your pain, but they can give you a gentle source of healing and comfort vibrations to help usher through such difficult times. Some crystals can bring you inner strength, while others can bring an ease of acceptance, and still others will bring you gentle compassion. While their powers vary, they all have the same goal of working towards helping you cope with the loss and find some peace of mind.

HOW LONG IT TAKES:
15 minutes
WHAT YOU'LL NEED:
Hawaiian black salt
Myrrh
Lapis lazuli
Amethyst
Aloe vera
Globe amaranth

Amethyst is a universal and powerful healing crystal, and it can greatly benefit someone experiencing grief. During the period of grieving, it is normal to feel anxiety, stress, and nervousness, making your day-to-day activities very difficult. Amethyst is created with immense heat and pressure, ever reminding you that something can be beautiful when stressed.

STEPS:

1. Cleanse and smudge a medium size jar with a cork. Charge the jar with your intentions; speak aloud three times:

My friend is the wind, my friend is the rain.
Ease my heart from grief and pain.
So it is and should be.

2. Place black sea salt in the bottom of the jar.

3. Continue layering materials according to their number from the bottom.

4. Place the cork in the jar.

5. Anoint the jar with chamomile oil or the essential oil that comforts you the most.

Grief Behind is Peace of Mind Spell

There is not one specific factor that drives individuals forward after a period of grief, or that holds them back. Most people who think of grieving rituals think of social displays of bereavement, such as "sitting shiva," funerals, wearing black for a certain number of days, etc. However, inner healing is necessary, so that a person can continue with their life and gain back their peace of mind. That is why I created the "Grief Behind Peace of Mind" spell.

HOW LONG IT TAKES:

15 minutes

WHAT YOU'LL NEED:

Neroli oil

1 quartz stone

1 bowl of water

3 tablespoons of salt

STEPS:

1. Cup the crystal in your strong hand. Visualize your grief and pain in your mind's eye. Imagine the pain and grief spilling from within you and through your body to your hand and into the crystal.

As you do this, speak aloud:

> *Grief is a passage,*
> *Not a place to stay.*
> *Calm my heart,*
> *So I can greet the day.*
> *So it is.*

2. In a counterclockwise motion, stir the salt into the bowl of water.

3. Add the quartz crystal to the bowl.

4. In a counterclockwise motion, swish the crystal and salt water around three times.

5. Leave the crystal in the water for ten minutes.

6. Remove the crystal and throw it as far away from you as possible.

Life is a Balancing Act Spell

Chapter Four contains a list of crystals and their associated chakras. The word chakra, in Sanskrit, means "wheel," in reference to your body's energy centers. The spinning wheels of energy correspond to specific nerve bundles and the major organs in your body. If you or someone you care about needs a spell for balance, make sure to review Chapter Four if you sense a blockage, imbalance, or physical or emotional issues associated with a specific chakra. This is the best spell for balance. Since there are over 100 chakras in your body, it's no wonder that we fall off kilter every now and then.

HOW LONG IT TAKES:
5 minutes for 7 days
WHAT YOU'LL NEED:
Crystals chosen depend on imbalance

STEPS:

1. Wear crystals as jewelry over your chakra locations.

2. Meditate with the crystals.

3. Keep a crystal somewhere on you (pocket, brassiere, belt).

4. Place in the corners of your bath.

5. Keep a crystal under your pillow or on your nightstand when sleeping.

Now I Lay Me Down to Sleep Spell

Spells manifest the best when cast with a clear head and intense focus on the objective you desire. The magic is within you, it doesn't happen on its own. So, when it comes to a good night's sleep, I highly recommend you combine your spell with some deep breathing, a spiritual bathing ritual, and some relaxation techniques. When you are ready, prepare your sleeping space, making it as comfortable for yourself as possible before you do your spell. Have your lights down low or light a candle. Change the bed clothes. I am always amazed at the difference in the quality of my sleep when it is on freshly cleaned sheets. If you have a lavender candle or lavender essential oil, let it dance around your room until you achieve a beautiful, calming effect. Finish everything you have to do, like going to the bathroom, and get ready for bed.

HOW LONG IT TAKES:

30-45 minutes, as needed

WHAT YOU'LL NEED:

1 smoky quartz crystal

1 snow quartz crystal

10 dried lavender stamps

1 sheet of paper (untreated if possible)

STEPS:

1. Sit in your bed in a comfortable position. Place your spell materials next to you.

2. Hold a crystal in each hand. Focus your intent on each crystal's energy and how it feels in your hands.

3. With your eyes closed, gently move the crystals around in your hands; notice every ridge and bump. Slowly feel them starting to warm up with your touch. Let their energy pass through your hands and throughout your whole body.

4. Turn your attention to the smoky quartz and feel its calming-grounding energy transforming all of your negativity into positive and peaceful sensations.

5. Send this energy down to your toes.

6. Turn your attention to your snow quartz and feel its hope radiating in your palms. Feel the snow quartz flowing through you.

7. Let yourself fall into the powers of the crystals and their protective energy.

8. Allow your mind to quiet.

9. After a moment, quietly chant:

Peaceful sleep come to me.
My spirit, my mind will now roam free.
Grant calm serenity tonight.
Tomorrow is a beautiful sight.
As it is and should be.

10. When ready, gently and slowly open your eyes. If you can still feel the energies coursing through your body, close your eyes again for as long as you need.

11. When you're ready, take the lavender sprigs and the crystals and put them on the piece of paper.

Wrap them up carefully and place the package on your nightstand.

12. Ease yourself down into your bed and warm yourself in the comfort enveloping you. Thank your materials and fall gently into a deep slumber.

Color Me Creative Spell

Being creative can be a bit tricky, as it seems to come and go. In my experience, creativity has a tendency to arrive at the most inconvenient time. It usually happens when I am trying to fall asleep or while I'm driving in heavy traffic; it then vanishes at the exact time I need it. Creativity is governed by the sacral chakra, which just so happens to govern our passion and pleasure. So, it should come as no surprise that creativity is derived from our pleasure and passion center. Using the mega strong carnelian crystal will open your creative powers, allowing you to feel more original and inspired in every area of your life. Carnelian works together with your sacral chakra, creating a highly creative and powerful energy. It wakes up your creative side, so that you can imagine and inspire all that is good in your life. The power of words with intent is amazing, so speaking your creativity into existence and amplifying it with your crystal will give you a quick and powerful spell.

HOW LONG IT TAKES:

30 seconds

WHAT YOU'LL NEED:

1 carnelian crystal

STEPS:

1. Cup your carnelian crystal in both hands and speak aloud three times:

I am creative, talented, and smart.
As it is and should be.

Over the Moon Water Recipe for Spells

Soak the amethyst and clear quartz crystals in the moon water. The really neat part about this dynamic duo is that the amethyst powerfully charges the moon brew and works especially well with any creativity spells. The clear quartz amplifies the whole spell. The crystals charge the water and the water charges the crystals. This enhances your psychic attributes and works wonders with dream magic.

HOW LONG IT TAKES:

30 minutes prep and 13 hours moon brewing

WHAT YOU'LL NEED:

1 clear quartz or moonstone crystal

1 amethyst crystal

The full moon

1 floating white candle

1 cinnamon stick

1 lavender-colored flower

A corked glass bottle

A pot for boiling (preferably cast iron or use your
cauldron)

A glass bowl

Cheesecloth, coffee filter, or strainer

Funnel

STEPS:

1. Wait for a full moon. It helps to know in advance when this will occur so you can get excited about what you are about to do.

2. On the evening of the full moon, put your cinnamon and flower in water and gently bring to a boil.

3. Strain the liquid in a tied off coffee filter or wrap the components in a cheesecloth before boiling.

4. Let the brew simmer on low heat for 30 minutes.

5. When it has cooled down, pour into a glass bowl. Strain the herbs if you didn't use a filter or cheesecloth.

6. At the stroke of midnight, take your brew outside and place it under the moonlight (so you can see the reflection of the moon in the water).

7. Place your amethyst and clear quartz or moonstone crystal in the center of the bowl of water.

8. Send your lit candle adrift in your brew. If you feel it's okay, meditate for a few minutes and leave it overnight.

9. The next morning, pluck out the cold wax.

10. Funnel the water into your bottle and cork it.

11. Thank the moon and your materials.

12. Enjoy!

I Think It's Time for a Change Spell

In every person's life, there comes a moment where they want to make some type of vital change. It may be losing weight, starting a new job, or improving your financial state. Casting this spell can bring on that change. Your timing for this spell is crucial. It has to be during a new moon because fresh beginnings are aligned with the new moon. The new moon's energy will help you to let go of your past. Moldavite is the stone of transformation, maybe because moldavite itself was created through an intensely changing process. It is the crystal to choose if you want to make a vital change in your life, or if you wish to have good luck while you navigate change.

HOW LONG IT TAKES:
Bath time + 30 minutes or until candle burns down
WHAT YOU'LL NEED:
1 moldavite crystal
3 white candles

Sea salts

Candles (red for love; green for money; orange for creativity)

Paper

Candle snuffer

Ribbon (same color as the candle).

STEPS:

1. Cleansing bath ritual. Fill the tub with warm water and sea salts. Light three white candles around the tub. The purpose of this bath is for calming yourself while preparing for your spell work, not to imagine the future.

2. Place your colored candle in front of you or on your altar. Write down your intention, describing your life post change. Do this in the present tense.

3. Cup your moldavite crystal in your hand and visualize and feel the positive emotions this change has in your life.

4. Fold the paper in a direction toward yourself, so the energy is directed back at you and place it under the moldavite crystal.

5. Scribe your intention on your candle. Either a symbol such as $$ or in words.

6. Light the candle.

7. Place the parcel and the Moldavite crystal so it is hit by the glow of the candle.

8. As you gaze into the flame, speak aloud:

I make this claim,
as I ignite this flame.
I embrace this change,
but self-love remains.
As it is and should be.

9. Either snuff out the candle or stay with it until it burns all the way down. You want to receive all of the energy from the charging Moldavite.

10. When the spell is complete, take back the parcel and unfold it. Roll the parcel that has your intention writing on it into the shape of a cylinder.

11. Take the cylinder and the Moldavite and put them together where they cannot be disturbed or ever found.

12. Your future is yours!

I'm Not Angry Spell

On any given day we can experience turbulence in our emotional landscape. Some days, I feel pushed and pulled in all the wrong places, anxious, overwhelmed, and every once in a while, downright angry. If this ever happens to you, and you don't want those feelings to hang around, cast this "I'm Not Angry Spell" as part of your handy self-care spell rituals. Anger stems from an unbalanced or blocked flow of your natural energy in the throat and root chakras.

HOW LONG IT TAKES:

Bath time + 30 minutes or until candle burns down

WHAT YOU'LL NEED:

Howlite

Peridot

Smoky quartz

Amethyst

Bloodstone

STEPS:

1. Meditate with any of the crystals above for anger releasing and to channel positivity into your life.

2. Hold sessions with your family, friends, or group and communicate while holding the crystal and it will help you get to the root of the problem.

3. Keep the crystal in your pocket. It is best if it is touching you at all times. So, wearing it in aring, or other type of jewelry is a great idea. Keep touching it so it can suck the anger right out of your mind.

4. Have a crystal where you feel the angriest. If you lose your temper at work, at home, or in any other stressful environment, let the crystal slowly rid your environment of all toxicity.

5. Place them around where you notice the maximum concentration of negative energy and conflict.

Begone Negativity Spell

Some think an illness or a disease is the reason for having fatigue or prolonged aches and pains, but have you ever considered that negativity might be either part of the problem or the cause of the problem? Negative thinking affects more than just your state of mind; in fact, I believe it festers into everything from headaches to heart problems and prolongs the recovery time if you are sick. Practice the "Begone Negativity Spell" to help you transform your negative energy into positive energy.

HOW LONG IT TAKES:

21 days

WHAT YOU'LL NEED:

Lepidolite crystal

Amethyst crystal

Blue lace agate

Moonstone crystals

Sage

Lavender

Juniper

STEPS:

1. Make sure your crystals for this spell are cleansed and charged.

2. Use the same method for cleaning your crystals that you use for your aura and your soul. Sage, lavender, and juniper, combined with amethyst, blue lace agate, or a moonstone grid can be used. Smudge your crystal and then your body from head to toe. Visualize all of the negative energy disappearing.

Cleansing Negative Energy Spell

The color of clouds under a midnight full moon seems to transport me to the mystical world. A smoky quartz crystal is for the soul as a multivitamin is for the body. It stands ready to neutralize any negativity headed your way. It is your anchor in the storm of doubt. The smoky quartz will detox and purge the "stuff" that is deep down and glued to your aura. You don't want negative energy to fester and become denser in your physical body. Smoky quartz is a type of naturally irradiated crystal formed when the molecules are exposed to gamma-rays. The process is slow and completely natural. The crystal knows bad juju because gamma-rays are released into the earth from elements that are naturally decaying, such as uranium. So, this crystal soaks up any decaying energy in you!

HOW LONG IT TAKES:

21 days

WHAT YOU'LL NEED:

Smoky quartz crystal

Sweetgrass

Frankincense

STEPS:

1. Place the crystal on your altar with some sweetgrass and frankincense. If you need an instant cleaning and you are busy, simply hold the crystal and plants in your hands while you are working or tending to clients throughout the day.

Energy Boosting Spell

Most of us know the feeling of all our energy being drained; that overly-tired time of the day or night when no matter how alluring something seems, we cannot seem to get ourselves psyched-up enough for it. It's even more difficult to notice low-frequency energy drains, where you don't always experience the normal signs of fatigue. All you know is that you just don't feel that get-up-and-go energy for things you normally love. I lose my focus when I am experiencing periods of low energy, so I created this spell for me and you for those times when we need a bit more than a cup of java to feel good.

HOW LONG IT TAKES:

15 minutes

WHAT YOU'LL NEED:

Your favorite music

Rose quartz crystal

Vervain herb

Abalone shell

STEPS:

1. This spell is best done when you are by yourself, so you can turn up the music.
2. Select a song that makes you want to get up and dance, one that is uplifting and makes you want to swing your hips.
3. Put your vervain herb in the abalone shell and light it.
4. Place your rose quartz next to the smoking vervain.
5. Turn up the music.
6. Feel the energy flowing into your body from the charging rose quartz and vervain.
7. Off you go!

You've Got a Friend Spell

Friendships require mutual respect and continuous effort to keep them healthy. As time goes by and people mature, sometimes friendships can grow apart. If you are looking for a new friendship or you have a friend who is upset with you, this spell helps witches bond with new friends and improve the relationships with the ones they already have. I recommend doing this spell whenever you crave closeness.

HOW LONG IT TAKES:

12-24 hours

WHAT YOU'LL NEED:

1 bowl or dish of water (can be your moon water)

1 rose quartz crystal

1 blue candle

Rose oil

A waterproof item from your friend or a waterproof item you would gift a new friend

STEPS:

1. If this spell is to enhance a current friendship, get your friend's permission first. Trust is the foundation of any friendship, so you do not want your friend to ever think you were trying to manipulate them without their knowledge.

2. Put two drops of essential rose oil on the rose quartz crystal.

3. Put two drops of essential rose oil into the center of the blue candle.

4. Put the crystal into the center of the bowl.

5. Light the candle and place it next to the bowl.

6. Speak aloud:

I call on the power of the element of water to bind together candle, oil, and stone, as it will bind together my everlasting (new) friendship or friendship with (friend's name) in harmony. And it is done.

7. Snuff out the candle.

8. Place the bowl with the crystal under a waning moon overnight or leave it in overnight if you used your own moon water.

9. Take the crystal out of the water. You can save this water in a bottle and label it as a new *"The Moon is my Friend Blessed Water"* for rituals.

10. Give your item to your new friend or close friend whenever you feel distance. Hold it in your hand and tell your friend to do the same. Keep it in a place where you sit on a regular basis.

9

LOVE SPELLS

This chapter is going to cover issues surrounding unrequited love, finding new love, how to win over someone's heart and how to use the power of crystals to fill their mind with images of you! Let's say there is already a bit of chemistry happening between you and your love interest; manifesting a love spell will influence your love interest in a way that will make you the center of their thoughts and dreams. Love spells are crafted for differing circumstances and situations. That's why I have crafted the following spell to suit your specific needs. Therefore, you must take into consideration the primary purpose of the spell and why you use it.

Looking for Love in All the Wrong Places Spell for Wholeness

I am sure you've heard the song "Looking for Love in all the Wrong Places." Well, this is true if you are not looking within to find love. We want other people to deeply love us, when much of the time we are not practicing self-love! How can you possibly receive from someone else what you do not believe deep inside that you deserve from yourself? It is like being in a plane crash and putting the oxygen mask on another person first. For me, I feel quite disturbed by the thought of having to depend on love from outside of myself. Wouldn't it be nice if all the love you receive comes on top of your own self-love? That is why I have created this spell for wholeness ritual; it is to help you find yourself when you feel lost and to get to know yourself on a deeper level than you have ever experienced before.

HOW LONG IT TAKES:
15 Minutes
WHAT YOU'LL NEED:
Moonstone crystal
Black onyx crystal
Celestite crystal

STEPS:

1. Identify where you feel empty inside and choose a crystal. Maybe you're battling eczema or Crohn's disease, or maybe you feel lost and depressed and can't find the origin of your pain.

2. Focus on filling the void. Be specific and call it by name. Here are the crystals I usually use when I am not feeling whole:

3. Moonstone is the crystal of new beginnings and works for me when my stomach is tied in knots. Charge and anoint it and wear it around your neck.

4. Celestite is for a good night's sleep and lifting your mood. Keep it next to your bed, on a nightstand to feel calm and healed.

5. Black onyx will ground you. One of my best friends gave me a black onyx when I was leaving for college, and I gave one to my new roommate to eliminate negativity and bring peace.

6. Cleanse, anoint, and charge the three crystals. Since you are performing healing rituals, it is very important to rid your crystals of any negative energy. You can smudge them, clean them with salt, or rinse them with spring water. For healing and wholeness, you need fresh energy, not stale energy. Just the thought of a crystal being weighed down with stale energy is repugnant to me.

7. Set an intention to will yourself to be whole. If you are feeling down, hold the celestite crystal to the back of your neck or to

any part of your body that needs healing. Hold the black onyx to your forehead if you need to feel one with the earth. Know that you will be healed.

8. Whether you are new to energy healing or you are a fourth-generation witch, you can practice your intentions to manifest positive changes and improve your health.

My Eyes are Drawn to You and Yours to Mine Spell

It is important to cast this spell on a Friday, the day of Venus. Also, you want to cast this spell on a full moon or a new moon when love spells are most effective.

HOW LONG IT TAKES:

30 minutes

WHAT YOU WILL NEED:

1 pink candle

1 rhodochrosite

1 rose quartz

Palo Santo smudging bundle

Rose petals

STEPS:

1. The most important part of this spell is setting your intention. Imagine a clear picture in your mind of who, what, where, and when you want this love spell to work. This spell is for new love and works best when you have seen someone you

are attracted to and you want them to notice you back. Meditate on whether you are in a good place in life to enter into a relationship with your love interest. I know a few witches who cast a love spell only to wish that they had done it at a better time. For example, if you have children, you may want to wait until after summer break. Same, if you are a college student, you may want to wait until after final exams. Make sure to steer clear of any intentions involving manipulation, control, or domination.

2. Make sure to charge your crystals.

3. Place the crystals on each side of the candle.

4. Light the candle and move one crystal one inch clockwise and the other crystal one inch counterclockwise.

5. Do this once a day until the crystals touch each other.

6. Once they are touching, place them atop the rose petals and chant:

> *My heart and soul so filled with fire,*
> *Bring to me my heart's desire.*
> *Crystal of love shimmers so bright,*
> *I'm looking for true love tonight.*
> *So it is done.*

7. Blow out the candle and be patient. Carry the crystals together in the same pouch or pocket until the love you have been waiting for arrives.

Let's Talk Communication Spell

Do you wish you knew how to communicate better with your significant other(s); that you knew how to say what you mean before you say something that can cause a disconnect or conflict between you? Do you suddenly find yourself in the middle of an argument without knowing how you got there? Are you having difficulty explaining yourself or expressing your feelings? Good communication requires mutual respect and effective listening. I created this spell to help ease communication efforts, but you have to be willing to listen to your loved one without preparing a rebuttal while they are talking. If you are thinking about what you are going to say when the other person is talking, it is impossible to hear them. Stay calm, cast this spell, and then listen.

HOW LONG IT TAKES:

20 minutes

WHAT YOU'LL NEED:

1 blue candle

Lilac incense

Lapis lazuli crystal

Lavender buds

1 small dish

Amber oil

Abalone shell

STEPS:

1. This spell is best cast on your altar.

2. Light your lilac incense and wave over your lapis lazuli crystal to charge it.

3. Put your incense in your abalone shell.

4. Light your blue candle.

5. Put your lavender buds into the small dish and place the crystal in the center.

6. Rub the amber oil on your throat in a clockwise motion and speak three times:

> *Communication breeds trust.*
> *Trust is a must.*
> *I'll talk to you.*
> *You'll talk to me.*
> *Together with trust, we'll be.*
> *And so it is done.*

7. Let your candle burn down or snuff it out. Repeat this spell every day for three days.

Light My Fire Rekindling Passion Spell

We all want passion in our relationships; to feel a sense of adventure with our connections and intimacy. But sometimes the passion starts to fade and the relationship begins to suffer. Before you practice your magic, ask yourself what you believe has caused the stagnation. Maybe time has just gone by and the two of you now have more of a companionship than an intimate relationship. Is it one-sided? Or maybe you have both stopped putting the same effort into it that you once did because of kids, work, or age? Whatever the reason your excitement has waned, you now want to rekindle the passion, excitement, and lust you and your partner once had. This is a tried-and-true spell, so get ready!

HOW LONG IT TAKES:

90 minutes

WHAT YOU'LL NEED:

A sunny day

1 orange carnelian crystal

1 rose quartz

2 red candles

Red cellophane

1 elastic band

1 glass of water

Rose essence

1 red rose

STEPS:

1 .Put your rose on your altar in some water.

2. Put a few drops of rose oil on both crystals.

3. Put the crystals at the bottom of a bowl.

4. Place the bowl on your windowsill, letting it get sunlight for one hour.

5. After dark, put the candles in the middle of a table and light them.

6. Gaze into the candles and think of you and your partner becoming one in unity.

7. Put one drop of rose oil on two rose petals and float them in the bowl with the crystals.

8. While gazing at the candles for three minutes and thinking about passionate closeness, chant the following aloud three times:

> *Crystals and candles together ignite.*
> *Bring alive our passion tonight.*
> *Desire between us will be true.*
> *Some passion for me and some passion for you.*
> *Let it be done.*

9. Burn the candles for one hour and then snuff them out.

10. Sleep with the crystals under your pillow until the passion reignites.

11. Once it does, put them together on your altar for keeps.

It's Over: Letting Go of Lost Love Spell

Oh, the pain of letting go! It is just an awful feeling. Even when you know it is the best for both of you, tending to a broken heart is never any fun. However, it can be a very exciting time to set your intentions on self-care, self-awareness, and creativity. Here is a spell you can cast to bring in new beginnings and let go of your old ties when you find yourself nursing a broken heart.

HOW LONG IT TAKES:
One day
WHAT YOU'LL NEED:
A full moon
1 abalone shell
1 piece of paper
1 red ink pen
1 citrine crystal
1 aquamarine crystal
Scissors
1 red candle

STEPS:

1. Give back or give away all of your ex-partner's belongings. Items hold energy, so it is imperative that you clear that energy. If you have to, get a close friend to return the items to your ex, and whatever that person doesn't want back, get rid of. You can always donate items.

2. A full moon is the best time to set your letting go intention.

3. In red ink, write down the person's full name.

4. Fold up the paper.

5. Go into your backyard or somewhere you can place the crystals under the full moonlight.

6. Take the scissors and cut the parcel in two.

7. Place ½ under the citrine crystal and ½ under the aquamarine crystal.

8. Leave them there overnight.

9. Bring the pieces of paper and the crystals to your altar.

10. Light your red candle.

11. Burn both pieces of paper with the ashes in your abalone shell.

12. Collect the ashes in your shell and snuff out your candle.

13. Bury your crystals in the ground either on the side of a crossroad or in a field away from you.

14. Let the ashes blow away and say:

I believe it's best for you and me.
I release you now so I'll be free.
The relationship is gone,
I am moving on.
As it is and should be.

Desirable Me Spell

The simple truth here is that you ARE desirable with or without magic. But a bit of spell work can add to your fun. You are not like anybody else. If you haven't looked in the mirror lately, that might be part of the problem. No one can rival your desirability as long as you know it to be true. Of course, everyone has their own "taste" in what they consider desirable, but that is irrelevant. Everyone wants to feel desirable. There are days when I just can't even imagine anyone finding me desirable, and I am not talking about a bad hair day. I mean when my stress level is high and it shows. It happens to the best of us. That is when this spell really comes in handy. This spell is just to boost your feelings of being desirable because you already have everything you need. So, a bit of crystal charm will help you feel it!

HOW LONG IT TAKES:

11 minutes

WHAT YOU'LL NEED:

1 sunstone crystal

STEPS:

1. Sunstone is the crystal for desirability. It keeps our sensuality from hiding within and motivates us to bloom outward instead. This crystal holds within it the sun's revitalizing energy and has the power to forge brightness back into your life and affirm your truth that you are desirable and desired!

2. Hold the sunstone over your third eye, and say aloud:

> *I allow my inner glitter and radiance to shine through.*
> *I am desirable, I am anew!*
> *As it is and should be.*

3. Imagine yourself with a white glow radiating out of your pores, sparkling brilliant, and expanding with the light.

4. Put your sunstone by your dressing mirror for three days.

Faithfully Yours Spell

Trust and faithfulness are inherent and complex needs. We look to trust other people, and we want others to think of us as trustworthy. Most human interactions depend on mutual trust. However, some relationships often lack mutual trust. Much of the time we fear or lack trust in our relationships due to our own insecurities. I have noticed in my life, the more confident I am in myself, the less I worry about faithfulness in others. In this spell, you will be using blue crystals because they are tremendously helpful in overcoming insecurities. In almost every case I have ever known, unfaithfulness has torn apart relationships, making them seem nearly impossible to repair. The best way to avoid this heart-wrenching pain is to avoid infidelity yourself. If you are the one trying to stay faithful or keep your loved one faithful, use blue crystals. Sodalite and lapis lazuli work best for this spell.

HOW LONG IT TAKES:

5 minutes

WHAT YOU'LL NEED:

Licorice herb

Rosemary

Cumin

Sodalite

Lapis lazuli

1 dark colored pouch with drawstring

STEPS:

1. Scatter ½ of the licorice herb over your partner's footprints.

2. Put the other ½ of the licorice herb in the pouch.

3. Add some cumin to a meal you both eat at the same time.

4. Hold a crystal in each hand, chant the following, and then put the crystals in the pouch.

> *I trust myself and know the truth.*
> *I have the faith to trust in you.*
> *Our love is one that can't be beat.*
> *You nor I will ever cheat.*
> *And so it is and should be.*

5. Place all of the materials/ingredients in the pouch and put it under the side of the bed on which your lover sleeps and s/he will always be faithful.

Peaceful Endings Spell

For any witch wanting to replace the pain, confusion, stress, and hurt that comes along with the ending of a relationship (even if they are the one who wanted it over) with peace of mind, clarity, and tranquility for all involved, taking this cleansing bath ritual is the way to go. A witch friend of mine was headed to the dreaded divorce court after 11 years of marriage. They had one child who was eight years old. It was an awful time for everyone involved, but it was better than staying in an unhappy situation. She said this spell changed her, to the point that the whole family practiced it once a week during the difficult time and the couple peacefully and amicably separated.

HOW LONG IT TAKES:

30-45 minutes

WHAT YOU'LL NEED:

1 rose quartz crystal

5 drops of lavender essential oil

4 drops of rose essential oil

3 drops of rosemary essential oil

1 cup Epsom salts

½ cup coarse Himalayan pink salt

STEPS:

1. Place all of your ingredients into a potion jar, including the rose quartz crystal.

2. Infuse the potion with your positive intention by holding your hands or wand over the potion. Imagine peaceful love flowing from a never-ending source within your heart, down your arms, into your hands, through your fingers, into your wand, and into the potion of salts.

Interloper Be Gone Spell

Sometimes it is very necessary to remove negative people who just don't seem to get the message. It is not always that they are negative in their own right. Sometimes, their involvement in your affairs is what creates negativity in your life. I had a friend who was a bit down on his luck, going through a tough breakup. He had lost his job and was having a great deal of anxiety. Of course, I wanted to help and invited him to stay with me, for what in my mind was going to be a week or so. I did everything I could to ease his suffering. I don't think I ever put my wand down and my crystals were starting to grow heavy. I just couldn't seem to tell him he had to leave.

After a month, he was still on my couch. It was driving me nuts. I had finally had it. I very gently and kindly said to him, "I think it is time for you to move on and find a new place where you can be happy." He said he agreed, but then another week went by and it was as if the conversation had never happened. In this case, I could not ask his permission to do magic to get him to leave. But I did tell him I would cast a spell wishing him better times. And so I did. Two days later, another friend of his invited him to Florida. Happy days were here again and I didn't have to worry about any karmic backlash. Here is the spell, just in case you find yourself in a similar predicament.

HOW LONG IT TAKES:

15 minutes

WHAT YOU'LL NEED:

Black obsidian tumblers

1 black candle

1 piece of paper

Pen

1 bowl

STEPS:

1. Write the full name of the person on the piece of paper.

2. Place the black candle in the center of the bowl.

3. Create a sacred barrier around the candle with the black obsidian tumblers.

4. Light the candle and chant while burning the piece of paper:

Crystal of black; this candle burns slow.
From my life (name) must go.
As it is and should be.

5. Snuff out the candle and bury the crystals away from your home.

6. Throw away the candle.

10

PROSPERITY SPELLS

Financial prosperity is an important aspect of our lives but is far from easy to achieve. Many people fall into debt, dislike or hate their jobs, or can't even hold down a job. Sometimes it seems like there is no end in sight, only endless days of labor just to make ends meet. There is absolutely nothing wrong with the desire for money. If you are struggling, it is only because you have to learn how to attract money; rituals will help you to do just that. Every person is concerned with becoming financially independent and enriching their lives and the lives of those they love. You would be surprised how many wealthy people in this world consult witches, fortune tellers, and psychics before they conduct their financial transactions. The most common wish when it come to money is "to make it." That, right there, often calls for magic.

Debt Relief Spell

If you are down on your luck and your debt is piling up, use this debt relief spell and watch your debt disappear. Practical steps must also be taken, obviously. This spell works in two ways; one is magic and the other is to help you to be mindful when it comes to your finances.

HOW LONG IT TAKES:

25 minutes

WHAT YOU'LL NEED:

Photocopies of your bills

1 peridot crystal

1 malachite crystal

1 green aventurine crystal

1 black candle

1 cauldron

STEPS:

1. Place the black candle in the center of your cauldron.

2. Surround the candle with the crystals.

3. Tear up the photocopies of your bills into tiny pieces.

4. Light your candle and imagine all of your debt burning down to ashes. Chant 13 times:

> *This spell is to make me free of debt,*
> *No more over money will tears be wept.*
> *As it is and should be.*

5. Place the crystals and ashes into a paper bag and bury the bag away from home.

Monetary Magic Spell (Draw Money)

Monetary spells are a part of white magic. Like all white magic, money spells are cast to decrease the weight of negative aspects associated with finances, and increase the positive aspects. This spell will attract financial gains into your life. Believe me, money will come. However, don't expect to win the lottery the day after you do this spell. You will come into abundance, though, such as a hike in pay, a new, high-paying job, or an unexpected monetary gift. It is hard to tell how the spell will be manifested, but it will be manifested in the form of money.

HOW LONG IT TAKES:
10 minutes
WHAT YOU'LL NEED:
Full moon
1 green aventurine
Green or silver cloth

Tea Tree essential oil

1 silver coin (a silver dollar would work great)

STEPS:

1. Sit under the moonlight with your silver or green cloth on the ground.

2. Place your silver coin on your cloth.

3. Place your green aventurine crystal on top of the silver coin.

4. Gently wave your wand or your hands over your crystal and coin, while visualizing yourself picking up all of the silver the moon has spilled.

5. While you see yourself picking up all of the money, chant aloud:

Thank you spirit of the moon,
For bringing abundance to me so soon.
You filled my pockets over with silver
And now the gold will flow like a river.
As it is and should be.

I Have Confidence in Me Spell

How many times in your life have you passed up an opportunity because you were so sure you either didn't deserve it or there was no chance you would be able to achieve it? Have you passed up chances to invest in your own small business or travel on a whim? Are there times you wish you had spoken up, but were too afraid of other people's reactions? After today, you can leave your insecurities and doubts behind and radically change your attitude. Going forward, you will be confident enough to be the captain of your own ship of life, thanks to a bit of magic, a few powerful crystals, and willingness with intent.

HOW LONG IT TAKES:

5 minutes at night and 15 minutes the next morning

WHAT YOU WILL NEED:

1 hematite

Plain or stationery paper

Cinnamon

1 brown candle

1 rose quartz

Ginger

Thyme

1 pink pen, marker, or pencil

STEPS:

1. Write down eight (the lucky feng shui number) positive affirmations with your pink pencil, such as, "I am confident," "I am wonderful," and "I am strong."

2. Place all the other ingredients inside the paper and fold it up, so that the crystals, ginger, and thyme are on the inside.

3. Keep it next to your mirror or wherever you get dressed in the morning.

4. In the morning, light the brown candle.

5. Sprinkle cinnamon over the top of the candle and light it while chanting:

> *Burning candle, lovely wind,*
> *Bring me confidence from within.*
> *I'm calling for courage from above.*
> *I cast this spell for strength and love.*
> *So it is as it should be.*

6. Keep the parcel with the crystals inside until you don't need it anymore.

Get a Job Spell

These days, getting a job isn't easy, especially one that you will look forward to going to every day. Thanks to spells that work by the law of attraction, coupled with your commitment and energy, all the intention you will be putting into this spell will give you what you need to get that job offer you have been waiting for. Luck, work, prosperity, and good fortune will find you, and you'll be blessed.

HOW LONG IT TAKES:

1 week

WHAT YOU'LL NEED:

Waxing crescent moon

1 green aventurine crystal

Clove essential oil

Rice

Bay leaf

Sea salt

1 dish

STEPS:

1. Wait for a waxing crescent moon. Set your altar or cast your spell on the ground.

2. Make a circle of protection. Using sea salt, make a circle on your altar or on the ground around you for protection.

3. Set your intentions for a job into your rose quartz or tiger's eye crystal.

4. Put two drops of clove essential oil onto your crystal.

5. Place the crystal on your dish.

6. Add about a handful of rice and put the bay leaf on top of the rice.

7. Wave your hands or your wand over the dish and chant:

Bring to me this job I need
I'll do the work--I'll do the deed
The doors will open wide for me
As things will be as they should be

8. After one week, remove the crystals and keep them near you until you get the job.

You're Promoted Spell

This spell will help get you the promotion for which you have been working so long and hard. Sometimes, a bit of a crystal magic boost is just what the higher-ups need to put pen to paper, landing you that well-earned promotion. Casting this spell can bring words of praise your way, along with a raise in pay. Sometimes, the result of this spell may even be a new job offer. Take all things into consideration when projecting your intention into your spell.

HOW LONG IT TAKES:
45 minutes
WHAT YOU'LL NEED:
1 citrine crystal (charisma)
1 amethyst (wisdom)
1 sunstone (career success)
1 handheld bell

STEPS:

1. Cast a sacred circle or circle of protection.

2. Arrange your three crystals on the circle's edge with the sunstone crystal at the northernmost point.

3. Place the other two crystals according to your intuition in the southeastern and southwestern points.

4. You should be able to visualize a triangle with equal sides, with each crystal at each point of the shape.

5. Stand in front of the sunstone (northern) crystal with your bell.

6. Ring the bell three times loudly and chant:

> *May the powers of wisdom, charisma, and job*
> *success*
> *Grant me a promotion and my career be blessed.*
> *As it is and should be.*

7. Imagine your boss or higher-ups congratulating you on your promotion as if it already has happened, raise your arms over your head and chant:

> *I cast my intention for a promotion into the*
> *universe.*
> *May the spirits of luck, good fortune, and*

perseverance look upon me with favor. As it is and
should be.

8. Walk around your circle three times, again, but in a counterclockwise fashion; open your circle. Chant:

The spell is done and the circle is open.
May the universe bless my intention for a
promotion.
As it is and should be.

9. Pick up your crystals and put them near you at your workplace, touching them frequently until you receive your promotion.

Spell to Help You Focus

Sometimes there just aren't enough hours in the day. It's all hustle and bustle. But the ability to focus is critical to your success if you want to move ahead, learn new skills, be a better partner, and to anything else you need to do. When you lose focus, mistakes can be made and the quality of your work suffers. It is harder to solve problems and everything seems frustrating. This is when your crystals can help. For improved focus, unblocking your upper chakras does the job.

HOW LONG IT TAKES:

20 minutes

WHAT YOU'LL NEED:

1 hematite

Rosemary

Peppermint essential oil

1 cup or saucer

1 yellow candle

STEPS:

1. Smudge the hematite crystal with sage.

2. Lay the rosemary in the cup and put the crystal on top.

3. Put two drops of peppermint oil on the crystal and the candle.

4. Light the candle.

5. Hold the hematite in your hand and chant:

This crystal will help me with focus and memory as I work/study (name your endeavor for the following week).

6. Snuff out the candle and pass the hematite through the smoke and say:

As it is and should be.

7. Carry the hematite crystal and anoint your wrists with peppermint because it stimulates the same area of the brain as caffeine.

Business Success Spell

There is a lot going on in the world and businesses are struggling more than ever. But with the right energy, focus, and a bit of crystal magic, you can embrace your success in business whether you're new or you are already established yourself. Business is business, and you want to be successful. I am going to share with you a spell that will improve your business endeavors and raise your vibrational frequency at the same time. This will help you to cope with the stressors of being in business.

HOW LONG IT TAKES:
25 minutes
WHAT YOU'LL NEED:
1 citrine
1 green or gold sachet bag
1 piece of paper
1 green ink pen

Basil

Bay leaf

Orange zest

Gold or green thread

1 sewing needle

1 green or white candle

3 silver coins

Red rose petals

STEPS:

1. Start your spell in a peaceful room and meditate in a sitting position for a few minutes.

2. Put the bay leaf, basil, orange zest, coins, and citrine crystal into the perfume bag.

3. Write your intention on your paper in green ink. Be very specific: "I will have success in my business ventures."

4. Draw your business logo (if you have one) or any symbols of prosperity and success on the paper.

5. Fold up the paper into a parcel, put it in the bag and close the bag.

6. Hold your sewing needle over the candle flame while chanting your intention three times.

7. Sew your spell bag shut.

8. Do not blow out your candle, snuff it out.

9. Keep your charm bag with you or put it in your workspace.

10. When important business transactions or transitions take place, light your candle for a few minutes and then snuff it out, repeating your intention again.

Victory, Victory, Victory Spell

One of my favorite things about magic is that it is proactive! I just love this aspect of spell casting. Being proactive is the way to do the happy dance of victory. Getting the right crystals, keeping them cleansed and charged, keeping a sacred space, and knowing how to create a protective circle are all essential. These are all crystal-guided pathways to victory. I also love this spell. There is something very powerful about a clockwise spiral. Not sure why, but it resonates with me on a deep level and I think it will do the same for you.

HOW LONG IT TAKES:
15 minutes
WHAT YOU'LL NEED:
1 aventurine
1 hematite
1 pen
1 piece of gray or silver paper
Allspice
Cumin

Garlic

Basil

Ginger

Onion

1 abalone shell

STEPS:

1. Write the word "victory" on the piece of paper.

2. Draw the counter-clockwise spiral or the Irish victory symbol seen below.

shutterstock.com · 1052143982

3. Fold up the paper and put it in the abalone shell.

4. Place both crystals on top.

5. Add the herbs on top.

6. Chant the following words eight times:

Crystal of power, crystal of might,
Grant me victory here tonight.
Crystal of power, crystal today,
Victory, victory, I am here to say.
As it is and should be.

7. After three hours, grab the crystals and keep them on your altar or near your bed.

Legal Eagle Mojo Bag Spell

When it comes to legal issues, we either want to avoid them at all costs, or beat them at all costs. You want the results to be in your favor and any accusations taken away from you. This is where magic comes in. With the right spell, you can move things closer or farther away. This mojo bag is great to have around, just in case.

HOW LONG IT TAKES:

45 minutes

WHAT YOU'LL NEED:

1 drawstring bag

1 pen

1 piece of paper

3 hematite crystals

1 very small hematite

3 nails

Red string or thread

Sage clippings

1 drop of mugwort oil

1 vial court case oil

My Court Case Oil Recipe:

1/8 cup of almond oil

4 drops lavender oil

3 drops patchouli oil

Infuse with very small hematite crystals placed in the small sacred oil container

Store in a cool and dark place

STEPS:

1. Prepare my court case oil ahead of time.

2. Write your intention on a piece of paper.

3. Anoint three hematite crystals with the oil.

4. Tie red thread or string around the nails.

5. Put all ingredients into the pouch.

6. Carry with you until court date or when dealing with any legal issues. It is important that you **don't** take the mojo bag

into any government buildings as the nails will set off metal detectors!

7. Anoint your wrists with the oil before any legal situation and state to yourself, "as it should be."

Lucky Numbers Spell

Wouldn't it be nice if we had a spell for the lottery? I often wonder if any lottery winners practice magic. Simply given the law of odds, you would think some do. However, there is much to think about when it comes to numbers and magic. People tend to choose numbers they believe are lucky. That is the same thing as believing in magic. I often ask naysayers of magic if they have a lucky number. They almost always do. Oddly enough, they don't see the irony. Let's learn this spell.

HOW LONG IT TAKES:

30 minutes

WHAT YOU'LL NEED:

6 green aventurine crystals

1 green candle

Chamomile powder

Extra virgin olive oil

2 dice

1 green ink pen

1 piece of paper

1 penny

STEPS:

1. Mix one drop of olive oil with chamomile powder and rub into your hands. Repeat this before gambling.

2. Draw a four-leaf clover on a piece of paper and put four 7's in a circle around it.

3. Place in the center of the table.

4. Put the penny on top of the paper.

5. Put the candle on top of the penny.

6. Place the green aventurine crystals around the candle.

7. Put the dice on your favorite numbers and put them inside the circle.

8. Light the candle and say:

> *I cast this spell before the dice, powers that be,*
> *make my win nice.*
> *As it is and should be.*

9. Snuff out the candle, put your betting shoes on and good luck!

11

PROTECTION SPELLS

The fact of the matter is, when it comes to protection spells, every home and item in the home contains energies that you or someone has brought in. It may be a purchased item or a gifted item. However, it always has its own energy. Usually, energies are neutral or good, however, they can also be negative. Sometimes, bad things happen while items are in our possession. We don't want to throw away certain things that are either expensive, have been in the family a long time, or have some other important meaning. I have come across random items that just seem to cover me with an ominous feeling, and I am not sure why, but I am sure it is a case of negative energy! This chapter will cover how to protect yourself, your home and office, your car, and any other possession you have.

Sacred Boundary Protection Spell for Your Home

In my years of practicing magic, I have counselled many on spells that can be cast to ensure protection for people, property, and homes. In reality, protecting the home is one of the more popular uses for magical work. Home protection spells have been cast since the ancient Egyptian, Greek, and Roman times, and they are cast all around the world. This spell is the one I feel is the safest, so I am happy to share it with you. This spell should forever protect your home.

HOW LONG IT TAKES:

3 days

WHAT YOU'LL NEED:

1 black tourmaline

1 citrine

1 rose quartz

1 fluorite

1 clear quartz

3 large nails

1 black candle

1 bulb of garlic

Water

Wine

1 bowl

STEPS:

1. Smudge, cleanse, and fill your crystals with your intention to protect your home.

2. Peel some of the garlic skin and lay under the iron nails.

3. Place the three nails in a bowl in the shape of a triangle on top of the garlic skin.

4. In the center of the triangle, place the clear quartz.

5. Place the other three crystals at the points of the triangle.

6. Sprinkle it with the water and wine.

7. Do this for three days.

8. On the fourth day, throw the crystals out into your yard and drive the nails into the ground.

9. Chant:

As it is and should be.
Privacy Please Spell

It can be very challenging to have to put up with negativity in our life, especially when it comes in the form of a neighbor. After working all day, coming home should be an opportunity to rejuvenate and to have some privacy. Nosy neighbors or even friends can really put a damper on relaxing in your home. After all, no one wants neighbors who project negative energy into their homes.

HOW LONG IT TAKES:

25 minutes

WHAT YOU'LL NEED:

1 bowl

1 selenite

1 smoky quartz

1 black tourmaline

Olive oil

Chamomile leaves

STEPS:

1. Cleanse your crystals thoroughly.

2. Roll them in the olive oil and then the chamomile leaves and put them one at a time in your bowl.

3. Speak your intention aloud for each crystal.

4. Write your intention on a piece of paper and tuck it under the black tourmaline crystal.

5. With your palms facing the crystals, imagine sending white light toward them.

6. Ask the universe for privacy, safety, friendliness, and positive relationships with all of your neighbors and the rest of your community.

7. Speak this chant:

> *This spell I cast is for privacy today*
> *To make nosy people go away.*
> *No harm intended to see this through.*
> *It's only solitude I pursue.*
> *As it is and should be.*

Have a Safe Trip Spell

Right up there with protecting yourself and your home, spells for safe traveling are some of the more popular spells to cast. If you think about it, many people have some form of protection charm hanging from their rearview mirror or in the glove compartment of their vehicle, in a pocket, or in a suitcase. We have all types of spells for personal space and home protection, but we need spells like this one for when we are away from our home or traveling.

HOW LONG IT TAKES:
10 minutes
WHAT YOU'LL NEED:
1 bowl
1 smoky quartz crystal

Dried mint

Comfrey root

1 4-inch square of blue fabric

White string

STEPS:

1. Place the bowl next to your open suitcases.

2. Hold the smoky quartz in your dominant hand.

3. Light the dried herbs.

4. Wave the smoke over the suitcase.

5. Zip the crystal into one of the inside compartments of your luggage.

6. Repeat steps 1-5.

7. Tie the crystal into the blue fabric.

8. Walk around your car three times with the crystal package, imagining a protective barrier around it and chant:

> *I am going there, as I am here;*
> *my travel is safe, my road is clear.*
> *I cast this spell to guard my car.*
> *It runs well and can travel far.*
> *As it is and should be.*

9. Put the enwrapped crystal in your glove compartment.

Mental Block Removal Spell

I want to issue a word of caution with this spell. There are several crystals that are very useful in removing mental blocks. It has been my experience that, sometimes, crystals can unblock issues that you may not be ready to deal with. Therefore, I would suggest beginning with a crystal that manifests in a more subtle manner, such as a rose quartz. This will only set free issues you are ready to accept and move beyond. Next in strength, perform your ritual with lapis lazuli to remove blockages that were hiding the truth from you. When you're ready, malachite unblocks deeper emotional issues and may leave you in tears. Lastly, obsidian can be used to blast through the rest of your blockages. This may leave you temporarily bewildered.

HOW LONG IT TAKES:

It varies

WHAT YOU'LL NEED:

1 rose quartz

1 malachite

1 obsidian

1 lapis lazuli

STEPS:

1. Wait until sunset or midnight.

2. Create a sacred circle.

3. Focus on your intention to remove mental blockages.

4. As the sun goes down, chant:

> *As the sun goes down or as midnight reigns, my*
> *mind is free.*
> *Clear all mental blockages from me.*
> *As it is and should be.*

5. Repeat the chant several times or until you feel the blockage is removed, and when you're ready move to the next crystal, repeat the steps.

Banishing Spell

Banishing should be considered an almost natural skill for any witch to cultivate. It is a cornerstone of spell practice and was the first thing I learned as a new witch. Whether you are banishing a situation, a person, negativity, or an unwanted spirit, this spell is an important one to have in your witch's tool kit!

HOW LONG IT TAKES:

15 minutes

WHAT YOU'LL NEED:

1 apple

1 small obsidian

1 mint leaf

1 knife

1 skewer

Black ribbon

STEPS:

1. Write what you want to banish on a piece of paper.

2. Horizontally cut the apple in half.

3. Dig out the core of each half.

4. Rub one half of the apple with the mint leaf.

5. Stick the crystal and the piece of paper in the apple.

6. Skewer the apple together.

7. Tie the apple together with black ribbon.

8. Bury the apple in your yard.

Give Me Courage Spell

At some point in everyone's life, fear takes over and we can act cowardly. If you have ever seen the *Wizard of Oz*, you may remember that the lion lacked courage. But, if you noticed, he was the one who always showed courage. He just needed to believe in himself, just like the scarecrow and the tin man needed to believe in themselves... just like you or me. It is always our intention to be courageous, but every now and then, we need a bit of a magical boost to summon our courage from deep within.

HOW LONG IT TAKES:
20 minutes
WHAT YOU'LL NEED:
1 moonstone
2 yellow candles

STEPS:

1. Light the candle on the left and chant:

Candle on the left,
Guide me through my quest.

2. Light the candle on the right and chant:

Candle on the right,
Give me courage and might.

3. Hold the moonstone in the palm of your dominant hand tightly.

4. With your palm facing downwards, wave your hand over the top of the candles (be careful not to burn yourself) and chant:

From these flames of fire
and moonstone with desire,
it is courage, I admire.

5. For 60 seconds, with your eyes closed, imagine yourself in an act of courage. Play the scenario out in your mind to your desired result three times and chant three times:

I now have courage at the start.
I now have courage in my heart.
I now have courage in my walk.
I now have courage when I talk.
As it is and should be.

Children are Sacred Spell

All parents', witches included, number one priority is protecting their children. Guarding children from physical, emotional, spiritual, and emotional harm is the single most important aspect of a parent's life.

HOW LONG IT TAKES:
1 hour
WHAT YOU'LL NEED:
2 small rose quartz crystals

Super glue

White cotton

White cloth (approx. 1 foot)

1 lock of hair from the child or nail clippings/baby tooth

1 pen

1 piece of paper

Rose essential oil

2 cups of caraway seeds

White thread

STEPS:

1. Lay out your cloth and hand-draw a teddy bear on it.

shutterstock.com · 1482302564

2. It doesn't have to be perfect, but both sides should fit on the cloth because the front and back will be sewn together.

3. Write the child's or children's name on the paper.

4. Place two drops of rose oil on the rose quartz crystal.

5. Sew the front and back, leaving the top open for stuffing.

6. Fold up the paper and put it into some of the cotton.

7. Place the puppet to the side.

8. Put all of the items belonging to the child inside the puppet, then add the caraway seeds until it is full. It doesn't have to be stuffed to the seams. Caraway seeds have protective qualities.

9. Stuff the rest with the cotton.

10. Sew the doll closed.

11. Super glue the two small rose quartz to the cloth as the eyes. If you don't want to do that, place a rose quartz crystal on the inside of the doll.

12. Place your doll on your altar for three days. Three times a day, wave your hand or wand over it with your intention spoken aloud.

13. Put the doll in a hidden spot somewhere in the child's room but out of reach. Chant:

I hide you in (the child's name) room.
Guard this child with great stealth.
Protect this child from any dread.
Bless his/her health from toe to head.
As is it and should be.
Ward Off Illness Spell

We are all working diligently to stay healthy and avoid any type of illness. We also want to shield and protect our loved ones, especially those most vulnerable. So on top of practicing regular preventive care, I thought of this spell's intention to protect and ward off illness from any new diseases, and remove any new diseases from anyone visiting or staying in our home. It is both preventive and protective. I was led by a bit of folk magic and pure intuition.

HOW LONG IT TAKES:

1 hour

WHAT YOU'LL NEED:

1 clear quartz crystal

1 rose quartz crystal

1 amethyst

1 purple candle

1 picture of yourself or the person for whom you want to ward off illness

Chamomile tea

Lavender essential oil

Eucalyptus essential oil

Abalone shell or fireproof container

STEPS:

1. Prepare a sacred space with all of your materials in front of you.

2. Put your photo into the abalone shell or fireproof container.

3. Place your clear quartz crystal atop the photo.

4. Place the other crystals in a circle around the container in the form of a triangle with the amethyst at the top point.

5. Put a drop of each essential oil on the clear quartz crystal.

6. Anoint each crystal with a drop of each essential oil.

7. Light the candle.

8. Look into the fire of the candle and visualize yourself turning away any and all illness and pain, turning dark to light.

9. Close your eyes and picture a glowing protective barrier coming from the crystals and flowing around you or the person for whom you are warding off illness.

10. Visualize a glowing triangle surrounding the photo.

11 Chant:

I cast this spell to turn away
Any illness headed my way.
I am strong and healthy now.
I thank you spirits; I pledge my vows.
As it is and should be.

CONCLUSION

I hope you have enjoyed this exciting guide through the world of crystal magic. Crystals are powerful and versatile, loving, and mystical. They will protect you, bring you good fortune, and keep you company when you are feeling low.

With this book of crystal spells, you should be able to set your intentions and sharpen your magic in ways that will satisfy you and take to where you want to be as a new spell caster. If you were already experienced in the practice of magic, I hope that I have added wonderful new spells to your repertoire.

At this point, you have hopefully learned how to keep your crystals cleansed and charged, have some sacred moon water tucked away, and can cast spells ranging from love potions, good health and banishing to protecting your home and children and making more money!

Finally, it is my sincerest wish that you use this book to hone your own unique spell-casting styles using a wide range of crystals. I hope you learned how to keep your chakras balanced. Most of all, I hope that you have gained an understanding of the importance of intent and intuition. Like I always say, "as it is and should be!"

Get this additional book free just for joining the Hentopan Launch Squad.

If you want insider access, plus this free book, all you have to do is scan the code below with your phone!

CPSIA information can be obtained
at www.ICGtesting.com
Printed in the USA
LVHW021057040222
710250LV00002B/23

9 781736 656075